THE BOOK OF HIDING

The Book of Hiding offers a fluent and erudite analysis of the parallels between the Bible and contemporary discussions of gender, ethnicity, and social ambiguity. Professor Beal focuses particularly on the traditionally marginalized book of Esther, in order to examine closely the categories of self and other in relation to religion, sexism, nationalism and the ever-looming legacies and future possibilities of annihilation. Drawing from contemporary writers such as Cixous, Irigaray, and Levinas, Professor Beal challenges widely held assumptions about the moral and life-affirming message of Scripture and even about the presence of God in the book of Esther. *The Book of Hiding* draws together a variety of different perspectives and disciplines, creating a unique space for dialogue, raising new questions, and reconsidering old assumptions.

Timothy K. Beal is Assistant Professor of Religious Studies at Eckerd College, Florida. He is the chair of the Reading, Theory, and the Bible Section of the Society of Biblical Literature. He is co-editor, with David Gunn, of *Reading Bibles, Writing Bodies: Identity and The Book* (Routledge 1997).

BIBLICAL LIMITS

We have to move beyond the outside–inside alternative; we have to be at the frontiers. Criticism indeed consists of analyzing and reflecting upon limits.
– Michel Foucault ("What is Enlightenment?")

This series brings a variety of postmodern perspectives to the understanding of biblical texts. It challenges the traditional field of bibilical studies and invites new partners, including critics of literature, gender and culture, to press the boundaries of a familiar – and unfamiliar – Bible.

EDITORS

Danna Nolan Fewell
Southern Methodist University, Dallas, Texas

David M. Gunn
Texas Christian University, Fort Worth, Texas

Amy-Jill Levine
Vanderbilt University, Nashville, Tennessee

Gary A. Phillips
College of the Holy Cross, Worcester, Massachusetts

ALSO IN THIS SERIES

Jesus Framed
George Aichele

Reading Bibles, Writing Bodies
Identity and The Book
Edited by Timothy K. Beal and David M. Gunn

THE BOOK OF HIDING

Gender, Ethnicity, Annihilation, and Esther

Timothy K. Beal

London and New York

First published 1997
by Routledge
11 New Fetter Lane, London EC4P 4EE

Simultaneously published in the USA and Canada
by Routledge
29 West 35th Street, New York, NY 10001

Typeset in Garamond by
Ponting–Green Publishing Services, Chesham, Buckinghamshire
Printed and bound in Great Britain by
Creative Print and Design (Wales), Ebbw Vale

British Library Cataloguing in Publication Data
A catalogue record for this book is available from
the British Library

Library of Congress Cataloguing in Publication Data
Beal, Timothy K. (Timothy Kandler)
The book of hiding: gender, ethnicity, annihilation,
and Esther / Timothy K. Beal.
(Biblical limits)
Includes bibliographical references and index.
1. Bible, O.T. Esther–Social scientific criticism.
2. Group identity–Biblical teaching.
I. Title   II. Series.
BS1375.2.B42   1997
222'.906–dc21   97–2288

ISBN 0–415–16779–5 (hbk)
ISBN 0–415–16780–9 (pbk)

To Sophie, Seth,
and Clover

A breeze brought him the smell of clover – the sweet-smelling world beyond his fence. "Well," he thought, "I've got a new friend, all right. But what a gamble friendship is!"

E. B. White, *Charlotte's Web*

"Beal's book is a splendid exhibit of the new place we are in, in Scripture interpretation."
Walter Brueggemann, Columbia Theological Seminary

"This is an important book, not just for Esther studies but also for feminist biblical criticism and for the newly emerging study of ethnicity in the Bible. With a remarkable methodological sophistication Beal moves criticism of the book of Esther beyond the simplistic debate concerning the value of Esther as a good or bad role model to a consideration of the unstable and problematic ways in which gender and ethnic identities are constructed and reconstructed, negotiated and renegotiated in the book."
Carol A. Newsom, Emory University

"Tim Beal's sensitive interpretation of the enchanting yet disturbing 'Book of Esther' is a gift to students and teachers of Scripture. Though the mystery of the 'hiding' remains intact, the characters emerge in a new light, weaving a story that responds to our need for enchantment."
Elie Wiesel, Boston University

CONTENTS

PREFACE

Often, the landscapes of biblical literature appear initially to be plain and simple. No shadows, no unfamiliar regions, no hidden depths. But the closer you look, the more complex they become. The book of Esther (in Jewish tradition, Megillah, "the scroll") is no exception. The entire text is only eight or nine pages long in most English Bible translations. I could hardly summarize it in less. (I recommend that anyone unfamiliar with the story take twenty minutes to read it before beginning the present book.) On first reading, it appears so simple, so straightforward. But attend to the text more closely, and the landscape becomes increasingly complex and difficult to map. New and haunting questions arise and old answers suddenly need to be reconsidered.

I read the book of Esther as a literary farce that highlights the impossibilities of locating and fixing the not-self, or other (specifically the woman as other and the Jew as other) over against "us." In theater and literature studies, a farce is a performance that plays on broad improbabilities and exaggerations; in the kitchen, a farce is a seasoned stuffing. The two fields of meaning are not as far apart as they might seem. *Farcir* means "to stuff," and a literary or theatrical farce is "stuffed" with improbabilities, accidents, and exaggerations. On my reading of the book of Esther, it is the *aggregation* of the many identity convergences, shifting alignments, ambivalences, and marginal locations in the story that leads, ultimately, to the profound *disaggregations* of other subjects and the order of relations of "us" and "them" upon which they rely. The story of Esther is, in this sense, farcical. It is stuffed with identity convergences, disaggregations, and complex, shifting patterns of character alignment.

My focus in this book is not so much on how self and other are defined as it is on how such definitions are always unstable and problematic. Specifically, I am interested in the ambiguities inherent in gender and ethnic identities, especially in representations of the Jew as other (the "other Jew") and the woman as other (the "other woman"), and how those ambiguities can be used to bring about radical social transformation. I argue that such ambiguities can ultimately be used to subvert the very politics of anti-Judaism[1] and misogyny that depend on these representations of otherness.

Following the Introduction, "Dislocating Beginnings," which opens the book with a critical reflection on my own problematic social location in relation to my focus and argument, the chapters in the book move back and forth between readings in Esther and readings in contemporary theory concerning gender, ethnicity, and social agency. Some chapters focus entirely on Esther, others focus entirely on contemporary theoretical writings, and still others include discussions of both. In the process, it is hoped that my readings in theory will open new windows onto the landscape of the book of Esther, even while my reading of the book of Esther sheds new light on the theory.

Chapter 1 explores the story of Vashti as a farce on royal male power and misogyny. As an opening to the book of Esther, this story also opens a critique of the very sexual/national politics that is being introduced. The royal law, which aims to write out the other woman, backfires on itself.

Chapter 2 approaches the book of Esther as a sort of palimpsest (a text written over an earlier, erased text) in which traces, or erasure marks, of the other woman Vashti can be read throughout the narrative that follows, especially in the character of Esther, who fills the blank space Vashti leaves behind. Traces of the other remain. They cannot be erased entirely.

Chapter 3 turns to feminist biblical criticism, from *The Woman's Bible* (1895; 1898 [in two volumes]) to the present. By approaching the Bible primarily as moral literature (along the lines of "images of women criticism"), feminist biblical criticism has often detracted from a more radical study of how gender identities are formed, and how these formations become problematic, especially when put into play along with other codes of identity such as ethnicity. There is a need for an approach that can draw greater attention to identity convergences and patriarchal instabilities such as those prevalent in the story of Vashti and throughout the book of Esther.

Returning to the book of Esther, Chapter 4 focuses on the convergence of the other woman Vashti and the other Jew Mordecai.

I show how the story of Mordecai's refusal to bow before Haman and the subsequent order for the annihilation of all Jews in Esther 3 closely parallels the story of Vashti's refusal to be the royal male's privileged other and her subsequent exscription in Esther 1. This convergence suggests a solidarity between the other woman and the other Jew. Also explored is Mordecai's identification with the eunuchs, who operate ambiguously and often subversively on the threshold between genders.

Chapter 5 engages the theoretical work of Luce Irigaray on the projection of the other woman, and ultimately moves beyond her strict focus on gender identity formation into questions of ethnic identity. As an innovation on Beauvoir, Irigaray emphasizes the male subject's *dependence* on the other woman as a fixed negative image, or benchmark, for his own self-definition. This suggests a fundamental insecurity in male identity – an insecurity that is evident in projections of *both* the other woman and the other Jew in Esther. This chapter closes with a reading of Esther's encounter with Mordecai (Esther 4). Reading this episode after reading Irigaray highlights Mordecai's highly vulnerable dependence on Esther, who no longer appears to be entirely in his control.

Chapter 6 puts the writings of the Jewish philosopher Emmanuel Levinas into conversation with three episodes in Esther 5 – two face-to-face encounters with the royal law, and the king's subsequent bout with insomnia – as a way of exploring questions of memory, hatred of, and desire for the other, and the impermanence of the written law (in the book of Esther and beyond).

Chapter 7 reads between the theoretical writings of Judith Butler and the more poetic meditations of the "Jewoman" Hélène Cixous, exploring the ways incompatible convergences between identity codes (such as gender, ethnicity, and class) can be exploited for political transformation and even subversion. The chapter concludes by highlighting the socially impossible convergences on the "Jewoman" Esther, especially her identifications with Persian royal law on the one hand, and with the other Jew and other woman who are marked for oblivion by that law on the other. This chapter prepares the way for a new reading of the final chapters of the book of Esther, which follows.

Chapter 8 shows how the written law to annihilate the other Jew once and for all is subverted by Esther's strategic "coming-out party" (Esther 7), at which time she uncloset her own convergence of mutually incompatible identities. Suddenly the other woman and the other Jew emerge within the palace walls, throwing a royal drinking party. This begins a series of reversals that finds the likes of Haman impaled on a stake, the king groveling after the will of Esther, and all of Persia "Jewing" in fear for their lives. Yet this final shoring-up of Jewish identity (and the annihilation of the enemy) cannot be read without a profound sense of irony. The last word in the book of Esther is ultimately inconclusive.

After drawing together the various threads of my analysis from throughout this book, "In Conclusion" discusses the implications of my work for the field of biblical studies and for broader discussions of identity, otherness, and social agency. This book then closes with reflections on the Jewish festival of Purim. The cross-dressings and masquerades common in Purim celebrations, I suggest, are life-size interpretations of the strange and wonderful haunted playground of Esther.

All translations of biblical texts are my own, and are based on the *Biblia Hebraica Stuttgartensia* edition of the Masoretic text.[2] All Hebrew, except in a few instances, has been transliterated as simply as possible, in order to make it more accessible to those who do not read Hebrew. My own text work owes much to certain scholarly precursors, especially Michael V. Fox, Kenneth Craig (whose book on Esther and the carnivalesque appeared too late to be incorporated into my work as much as it deserves), David J. A. Clines, and Sandra Beth Berg. It is a privilege to follow such fine scholarship.

I am glad to acknowledge the many colleagues, students, and teachers (all friends) who have helped me write this book. Special thanks go to Rebecca Chopp, Gene Tucker, Walter Brueggemann, Athalya Brenner, Deborah Krause, Claudia Camp, Shirley Davis, Greg Briggs, Maya Minkin, Brent Plate, Geraldine Kandler Beal, Clay Beal, Danna Nolan Fewell, and Gary Phillips for important insights, corrections, support, and challenge. Thanks also to Eckerd College for support at key points, and to the people at Routledge London, especially Richard Stoneman, Patricia Stankiewicz, and Coco Stevenson, for their careful editorial work.

I gladly acknowledge my particularly extravagant indebtedness to David Gunn, Carol Newsom, and Tod Linafelt for their thoughtful attendance to far too many versions of the manuscript. Together they may have written more in the margins than I have written in the body.

I also remember, with gratitude and longing, my friends in the Tel

Mac Theory Lunch and Praxis Breakfast group. I miss them. The best of my work bears their marks.

I dedicate this book to my best colleague and partner, Clover, and to our kids, Sophie and Seth, even as I myself am dedicated to them. There has never been a time in the life of either Sophie or Seth that I have not been obsessed with Esther. Clover might vaguely remember such a time. Thanks to each of you for understanding.

Finally, this book is written in memory of two people. The first is my grandfather, Richard Kandler, a body and fender union worker by trade, who began reading the Bible late in life ("I never knew you could find this kind of thing in the Bible!"), and who died while I was writing this book. From him I began to learn about his mother's brother, Emil (Seidel) Kossatz, who, it is now only rumored, was killed in the Holocaust. The second is Valborg Gomness Kandler, Richard's first wife and my mother's mother, who died tragically long before I was born but whose presence has continued to be felt, like Vashti's, through a next generation's story. Traces remain.

INTRODUCTION
Dislocating Beginnings

For the critic must attempt to fully realize, and take responsibility for, the unspoken, unrepresented pasts that haunt the historical present.
(Bhabha 1994: 12)

This is not the book I thought I was writing. I had imagined that the book I was writing would begin and end with a party, a drinking party, a victory party – with Purim, a festival celebrating Jewish survival in the book of Esther. I have loved Purim for some time, but always from some undeterminable distance, always from some relative distance: not being Jewish. Why I am drawn to Purim, and to the text that Purim celebrates, has something to do with this sense of distance. And this sense of distance, in turn, has something to do with why this is not the book I thought I was writing.

During the festival of Purim (literally "lots"), reverence, sobriety, law, and authority go into a slide. Farcical plays based on the Esther story, called *Purimshpiels*, are often performed which parody the otherwise accepted authority of teachers, rabbis, and long-revered texts. Purim is, moreover, a festival preoccupied with masquerade. People gather in costumes and masks to hear, amid a cacophony of noise-making, a public reading of the scroll. Indeed, rabbinic tradition (Talmud Megilla 7b) commands Jews to drink so much wine on Purim that they can no longer tell the difference between "blessed be Mordecai" (one of the story's Jewish protagonists) and "cursed be Haman" (the story's ruthless anti-Jew).

It strikes me that one reason why Purim is so preoccupied with themes of carnival and masquerade – with blurring identities and subverting traditional structures of authority and power – is that Purim is very close to the text. As a communal, liturgical interpretation, the festival of Purim highlights a particular preoccupation in

1

the book of Esther with the art and politics of identity, especially with the ambiguities of ethnic and gender identity, and with the problematics of political orders that are based on those identities.

In one sense Esther reads like a comedy, the heroine withholding her "true" Jewish identity from the vacuous Persian king as the tension builds, and then, at the crucial moment, turning the world inside out and upside down by her revelation – a revelation that takes the form of a "coming-out" party. Yet, although the tone can be playful, the game is dead serious. The winners end up with prestige, authority, big houses, and lots of jewelry; the losers end up dethroned, banished, disenfranchised, dead in a pile, or impaled on a stake. The risks in this game are indeed high, and they are invariably entangled in issues of ethnic and gender identity. For all its political import, however, identity remains slippery in Esther, and particular identities often turn out to be far more ambiguous and problematic than they initially appear. In fact, they are the points of instability, the oil spots.

This book is a meeting-place between the Bible, especially Esther, and contemporary discussions of identity and social agency. Specifically, I focus on ambiguities inherent in gender and ethnic identity, questioning the possibility of defining "us" and "them," self and other, and exploring ways in which those ambiguities can lead to political transformation. In Esther, a game of self-definition is played out over against woman as other (the "other woman") and Jew as other (the "other Jew"). But this book is not limited in its scope to that particular game. Rather, in this book, the meeting-place between Esther and current discussions of gender and ethnicity becomes a site for rethinking broadly relevant questions about the categories of self and other in relation to religion, nationalism, and the ever-looming legacies and future possibilities of annihilation. Esther is a story about identity in the diaspora, and so are many of the stories we tell today. If exile and the aftermath of ancient Israel are Esther's heritage, exile and the aftermath of Western civilization are ours.

Esther's name can be translated as a form of the Hebrew verb "to hide." אסתיר: "I will hide," "I am hiding."[1] In many ways the book of Esther is a book of hiding. So is this book, preoccupied with the possibilities of veiling, misrepresenting, masking, and closeting otherness; of being more than one appears when the "more" is too much for the system to bear, and could explode the order of relations between us and them as it now stands; of hiding the fact that we always exceed the identities that frame us, the categories that map

2

our bodies and thus locate us on the political atlas. Read in this way, Esther elicits a sense of hope grounded in failure: the failure of political strategies aimed at marking and consigning the other woman and the other Jew to oblivion. In Esther, sur-viving, or *over-living*,[2] such limits depends precisely on this failure, and this hoped-for failure is, in turn, grounded in the ambiguities and excesses of otherness.

But another book has been hiding between the lines of this book of hiding: a book not about the other woman and the other Jew, but about the self whose heritage has defined its own identity, problematically, over against them. Indeed, for me, writing about the former demands that I write about the latter, for to recognize the ambiguities in the one marked as other is to recognize the ambiguities in the self doing the marking.

As I mentioned before, the book I thought I was writing was to begin, and end, with a party, with Purim as a living, dynamic, communal interpretation of the book of Esther. Many (Jewish) people first encounter Esther at a Purim festival. Indeed, many of my college students know it only in the context of Purim, and have never read the text itself. So: the book would begin with the festival, highlighting its peculiar preoccupation with the themes of parody, carnival, and masquerade. Then the book would turn back to Purim's text, to the book of Esther, in a sense mimicking the experience of so many people, who first encounter Purim and then ask about its relation to the Esther of Scripture. But that approach would not be honest – "mimicking" is the right word. For I myself came to the festival of Purim only *after* coming, as a Protestant student in a Protestant seminary, to the book of Esther. So even if this book were to begin with a party, I had not. (Seminary is no party.) This was not easy for me to admit, and I wondered why. This has become a haunting question, and also a question of haunting, in the sense suggested by Homi K. Bhabha's idea of the "presence of a haunting" (1994: 12–18): it remains in certain ways out of reach and out of control ("unspoken, unrepresented"), but nonetheless calls for a kind of *responsible accommodation* which would open this book with a more self-reflective and self-critical posture.

To accommodate the presence of a haunting is to experience – in that moment – a kind of dislocation, a being dislodged or "unhomed" (Bhabha 1994: 9). Hauntings make us aware of our *betweenness*: between the present and forgotten pasts, between the here and forbidden theres, between the self and ostracized not-selves. So that one may become aware that there are traces of the other – the projected, the exiled, the erased, the written-out, the burned-away – in the here, the now, the I. Within the storied world of Esther there are certainly many betweennesses, points of convergence that suggest the ways subjects in the story exceed, or over-live, the limits imposed on them by labels of gender and ethnicity. But there is another moment of betweenness, another diaspora, the sign of yet another haunting, which demands that this book be opened differently than I had initially thought to open it. This is the moment of my reading. The book of Esther is indeed a book of haunting presences, but so is my discourse on it: haunted by presences that, when attended to and accommodated responsibly, do not allow me to find a comfortable, settled location from which to write. Protestant interpretive tradition is, I suppose, my most ostensible heritage. I am well versed in it. Its codes, its theologies, its canons, its allusions are all very familiar. Yet, like many others today, I am also aware of feeling profoundly not-at-home within that discourse. Esther highlights why many of us experience our Protestant heritage with such ambivalence, for to read the ancient text of Esther today is, paradoxically, to be haunted by more recent pasts which Esther could never have fully imagined, and in which Protestant Christian heritage is most deeply implicated: a long, violent history of anti-Judaism, which has reached unspeakable, unwriteable horror this century in the Holocaust.

COLONIZING THE BIBLE

For me, as a Protestant coming to Esther, responsible accommodation of such haunting presences demands a different beginning than the one I had imagined. To explore the problematic ways that otherness is represented, I have come to realize, one must explore the problematics of *self*-representation as well, because otherness takes form over against self, and self takes form over against otherness; and the closer one looks at that opposition, that "over against," the more elusive it becomes. Then another still small voice whispers a wonderfully unsettling secret: self intertwines with other and other with self. This, I believe, is an ethical moment – and even, dare I say it, a moment of revelation – opening to a new relation, a relation that attempts, even after failure upon failure, to accommodate the presence of a haunting.

Let me begin, then, not with Purim, and not even with the book of Esther, but with a self-critical exploration of a particularly problematic Christian interpretive tradition in which the Jewish Bible, especially Esther, has been treated as a kind of Christian colony, a dark continent into which images of the Jew are projected as quintessentially not-us. This interpretive tradition, which I read as analogous to colonial discourse, has been a powerful identity-shaping apparatus within modern Protestant Christianity, especially since Luther, and has simultaneously served to form an image of the Jew – especially the Jew in Esther – as that identity's ultimate vision of savage alterity.

Judaism and Jewish Scripture present a fundamental, yet almost always sublimated, dilemma for Christian identity. On the one hand, Christianity's own self-understanding depends on maintaining identification *with* Jewish tradition, claiming, for example, Jewish Scripture as its own Scripture, and Jewish history as its own history. The God of Israel is our God. The God who called to Sarah and Abraham calls us. On the other hand, Christian identity has been, at least for most of its history, defined as *different from* Judaism, and even over against it. This basic dilemma has led in Christian thought to various forms of supersessionism, according to which Jews are considered somehow to have forfeited their own heritage and heirdom to God's promises, and Christians have taken their place. In biblical studies, this kind of supersessionism, I suggest, plays out rather like colonialism: Jews have not managed their own scriptural territory rightly, and it is therefore the right of Christianity to take it over, renaming it "Old Testament."

Within this colonial discourse on the Old Testament/Jewish Scripture, Esther poses a particular problem. Christian theology has had a very difficult time knowing what to do with this text. Esther is treated as the most remote outpost in the Old Testament colony: exotic, savage, violent, difficult to reach, difficult to map, dangerous, perhaps irredeemable. A different kind of colonial discourse therefore has emerged in Christian (especially modern Protestant) Esther studies, in which interpreters link what is asserted to be the *Jewishness* of the text – an ironic assertion, as will be seen later – with what is asserted to be its ungodly immorality, and then repudiate both as quintessentially not-us. This link, between Jewishness and godless immorality, in turn, is networked into a larger system of anti-Judaism. Here, then, images of "Jew" and "Judaism" as quintessential other, or not-self, are projected onto the text, and onto the modern world, by interpreters (self-represented in terms of sameness, normativity, non-divergence). The other world of Esther is used in this discourse to build "our" identity over against it.

This story extends back at least as far as Martin Luther's (1483–1546) famous repudiation of Esther, along with 2 Maccabees, in his *Table Talk*: "I am so hostile to this book and to Esther that I wish they did not exist at all, for they Judaize too much, and have much heathen impropriety."[3] This terse expression of deep loathing toward Esther and Maccabees – which, by the way, are the bases for two Jewish holidays, Purim and Hanukkah respectively – makes an explicit link between "Judaizing," or "making Jewish," on the one hand, and "heathen impropriety" or "perverseness," on the other. That is, Jewish identity is tied to irreligious immorality. Beginning in the latter half of the sixteenth century, with the rise of European colonialism and an increasing obsession with the "savages" of new worlds, the epistemological linkage Luther makes here, between ethnicity and morality, will become a very familiar theme in Western European colonial discourse. Howard Eilberg-Schwartz (1990) has shown how European Jews have often been projected as the *savage other within* European civilization – a dynamic that Jonathan Boyarin (1992: 77–98) has described as a kind of colonialism. In this passage from *Table Talk*, however, Luther puts a particular spin on this dynamic, focusing projections of the other Jew onto the savage landscapes of the Bible – a territory he is actively remapping through a new translation that would come to shape not only the future of the Protestant biblical canon but also of modern German identity.

There are, moreover, ominous echoes in Luther's wish that Esther "did not exist at all": in another late work, *Concerning the Jews and Their Lies*, he proposed that Jews themselves be expelled, provided other measures – burning their synagogues, destroying their homes, confiscating their scriptures and their property, forbidding rabbis to teach, forbidding them to travel, and forcing them into physical labor – were ineffective. In fact, four centuries later at the Nuremberg trials, Julius Streicher, who was one of the most vehement Jew-haters and Nazi propagandists, claimed that Luther ought to be on trial in his place, because he was only putting Luther's recommendations into effect (Eckhardt 1974: 24). As he was led to the gallows after being convicted, he shouted "Purimfest!" Ironically, with this exclamation Streicher identified himself not only with Luther but also with Haman in the book of Esther, who is the architect of Jewish annihilation and who is ultimately sentenced to death on the very gallows he had built for the Jew Mordecai. Indeed, with the character of Haman, the book of Esther has anticipated the reactions of both Luther and Streicher without fully imagining the extent of annihilation that a twentieth-century Haman might carry out.

One finds moral evaluations of Esther's "Judaizing" tendencies that are very similar to Luther's in the purportedly scientific (*wissenschaftlich*) treatments of Esther from leading Protestant scholars of the nineteenth and twentieth centuries as well. The highly influential German Lutheran scholar Heinrich Ewald, for example, wrote of Esther that "Its story knows nothing of high and pure truths. In it we fall as if from heaven to earth" (1843; English trans. 1869: 197). Note how the language of Ewald's evaluation builds Luther's repudiation into a network of oppositions, with the result that Jewishness and moral impropriety are now linked also to ignorance, impurity, baseness, earthiness, and fallenness, as opposed to knowledge, loftiness, purity, truth, and heaven.

One of the strongest twentieth-century anti-Jewish repudiations is Lewis Bayles Paton's International Critical Commentary on Esther (1908a), which, in addition to being an impressively comprehensive critical analysis of the Hebrew text, contains some of the most scathing criticisms of the text's excessive "Judaizing." On the "moral teaching of the book," Paton writes,

> There is not one noble character in this book. Xerxes [King Ahasuerus] is a sensual despot. Esther, for the chance of winning wealth and power, takes her place in the herd of maidens who become concubines to the King. She wins her victories not by skill or by character, but by her beauty. She conceals her origin, is relentless toward a fallen enemy (7:8–10), secures not merely that the Jews escape from danger, but that they fall upon their enemies, slay their wives and children, and plunder their property (8:11; 9:2–10). Not satisfied with this slaughter, she asks that Haman's ten sons may be hanged, and that the Jews may be allowed another day for killing their enemies in Susa (9:13–15). The only redeeming traits in her character are her loyalty to her people and her bravery in attempting to save them (4:16). Mordecai sacrifices his cousin to advance his interests (2:8), advises her to conceal her religion (2:10, 20), displays wanton insolence in his refusal to bow to Haman (3:2–5), and helps Esther in carrying out her schemes of vengeance (8:9). All this the author narrates with interest and approval. He gloats over the wealth and the triumph of his

heroes and is oblivious to their moral shortcomings. Morally
Est. falls far below the general level of the OT., and even the
Apocrypha.

(1908a: 96)

He then concludes by repeating, with full approval, Luther's famous
repudiation (Paton 1908a: 96). Indeed, Paton's evaluation of Esther
is an unpacking of Luther's comment, building an entire network of
binary oppositions around Luther's linkage of Jewishness, irreligion,
and immorality. "Judaizing" comes to be located as an oppositional
term: over against morality, religion, nobility, and loftiness; associated with sensuality, greed, relentless violence, "wanton insolence,"
vengeance, baseness, and "heathen naughtiness." By associating the
characters with the book's *author*, moreover, who "gloats" approvingly over their moral baseness, Paton identifies and evaluates both
the characters (as moral models) and the book itself (as moral
literature) in pure negative terms.

Written less than a decade after the Holocaust, Bernhard W.
Anderson's well-known article, "The Place of the Book of Esther in
the Christian Bible" (1950: 32–43), is a classic attempt to revise earlier
anti-Jewish repudiations of Esther. This essay struggles with questions of Jewish identity via an apologetic discussion (addressed to
Christians on behalf of Esther) of the *place* of the book in the
Christian canon. The article revisits the question of what Christians
are to make of this Jewish book, and asks how they can possibly
develop a positive evaluation of it. The more profound and pressing
question, however, which persistently overshadows the more explicit objective, is: what are Jews and Judaism, and how can Christians and Christianity possibly relate to them? The significance of
this article in the present discussion is not that it overcomes the
heritage of Christian anti-Judaism in Esther studies – it does not –
but rather that it shows how profoundly entrenched this heritage has
become in Christian theological discourse.

The article begins with the statement, apparently taken as self-
evident, that Esther is *"an emphatically Jewish book* whose primary
purpose is the authorization and regulation of a *purely Jewish*
festival, Purim" (1950:32; emphasis added). The author admits that
this Jewishness, along with the book's "indifferent, if not cynical,
attitude toward Jewish religion" (32), makes it "most offensive," a
"discordant note ... in the ears of those accustomed to hearing
the Christian gospel" (32). Quoting Ewald approvingly on the fall

from heaven to earth (see above), the author writes, "Surely this book is of the earth, earthy" (32). He also quotes Luther's comment from *Table Talk* and suggests that, had Luther "followed his better judgment," he would have taken the book of Esther out of the canon proper and put it in the Apocrypha along with the Greek editions (33). Already a familiar system of oppositions emerges, identifying the book of Esther with Jewishness, absence of religion, discordance, and earthiness on the one hand, and opposing it as foreign matter to Christians, the Christian gospel, harmony, and heaven on the other.

At this point, however, with obvious concern over the horror of anti-Judaism recently displayed in the Holocaust, the author swerves from earlier repudiations and argues that Christians *must* recognize the book's Scriptural status as the Word of God. How can this be done? Although he does not put it in these terms, this recognition is accomplished by breaking down the set of oppositional differences described above, namely, by discovering the book's religious and theological dimensions. First, he turns to (and, ironically, identifies with) Haman's description of the Jews in Est 3:8: "One people diverges, scattered and divided among all the peoples in all the provinces, . . . and their laws are different from every other people, and the laws of the king they do not do." Based on this text, apparently taken not as Haman's political construction but as a straightforward description, Anderson suggests that "the barrier of the Law," which is a "wall of separation behind which Jews could maintain their historical identity wherever they were dispersed" (34), and which is deeply religious, is the cause for suspicion, hatred, and violence toward Jews. This barrier, he speculates, has brought about an action-reaction "chemical equation . . ., Judaism inciting persecution and persecution creating Judaism" (35). Jewish identity, in this sense, would be created by the pull of common religious observation on the one hand and the push of persecution on the other. Esther, the author proposes, is a dramatization of this dynamic (34). On the one hand, this argument at least partially blames the victim. On the other hand, it begins to problematize claims that Esther lacks a religious element, and thus begins to break down the system of oppositions with which the author opened his discussion.

The most profound problem for Christians, however, for whom Esther and Judaism are still assumed to be *other*, is more directly theological: the Christian God of the "Old Testament" identifies with this people by choice. That is to say, for Christians, contrary to all appearances in Esther, Judaism (Israel as chosen) cannot be separated from the Jew: "The Jewish problem rests fundamentally upon the inextricable connection between Judaism and the Jewish people" (35). As already noted, for Anderson, Judaism is a problem for Jews because it acts as a wall that both distinguishes them from others and engenders hatred. Judaism is a problem for Christians, too, however, because it means that Jewish identity is established and guaranteed by *God's identification with* and election of Jews. This is the "Jewish problem" for Christians. In the end, then, despite appearances in Esther, God cannot be separated from this "earthy" people, or this "earthy" book.

Thus what appears initially to be the case in Esther cannot be accepted: Esther is distinctively Jewish, even "earthy," *but* must have a religious dimension as well. That dimension is found by Anderson (1) in the "barrier of the Law", and (2) in the fact of their (providential) survival over Haman. This survival is most significant for Anderson, writing from a Protestant neo-orthodox theological perspective (commonly identified with Karl Barth), for it "testifies to the indestructibility of [chosen] Israel," which will be the means by which God will reconcile and save all creation. For Anderson, the image of the Jew as quintessentially other to the "new law" of the Christian Gospel is problematized by the crossover identification of the Christian God with the Jew. "Gospel" is defined *opposite* "Jew," yet that Gospel's God identifies *with* Jews. The resolution of this problematic entangling of otherness with sameness is essentially Hegelian: the spectacle of the Jew as oppositional other is ultimately exposed, under the cross, as a mere spectre. That is, it is a *provisional* specularization of the other Jew, a provision required for the salvation-historical journey through the wilderness toward the total-izing telos of the cross, under which all is unified. This Jewish book and the Jews in and behind it are alien, other, not-us. Yet within the overarching narrative frame of ever-advancing salvation history they must be embraced.

I discuss this article at such length for two reasons. The first reason is that it highlights the dynamics of projection and fixation of Jewish otherness so common in Protestant (especially theological) discourse on Esther even while it struggles to overcome the heritage of that discourse as a structuring principle for Christian anti-Judaism. For its author, as for Haman (Est 3:8), Jewish identity is presented as a form of oppositional difference within a dialectical logic of the same versus the other. The book of Esther is Jewish insofar as it is not like "us," and within the Christian canon, Esther, in all its Jewishness, comes to represent the antithesis of Christian identity. In this sense it is the not-us within the us (insofar as the Christian canon serves to define the boundaries of Christian identity). For the theologian, this base, earthy, carnal antithesis must ultimately be synthesized into the march of salvation history. Here in Anderson's article, then, is a theological version of Hegelian dialectical thinking with regard to Christian identity and the Jews:[4] the Jew appears as other, antithesis, a negative image, and the book of Esther makes the Christian aware of this by its "offensive" and "discordant note"; yet the Jew is necessary for the March of History toward its great telos of full emancipation, at which time all will be revealed, redeemed, and fulfilled. To get to the promised land, one must brave (tame, assimilate, annex) this "uninviting wilderness." Moreover, from this perspective, one can recognize the divine Spirit at work, even and necessarily in Esther. Thus, by the Jewish other the Christian will be saved. Ironically, of course, in the final telos, "under the Cross," according to this theological-historical frame, the distinctive "place" and identity of the Jew will eventually evaporate – or, perhaps, totally "diasporate" – as will all oppositional differences (Gentile/Jew, male/female, heaven/earth). In a strange way, then, after showing how the oppositional encodement of Jewish identity with which the author begins cannot ultimately hold, he nonetheless allows it to hold for the moment, and hopefully defers its undoing to an indefinite future. A classic dialectical slight of hand.

The second reason for focusing on this particular interpretation is autobiographical. This article and the other interpretations I have discussed represent a mainstream of my own interpretive heritage as one raised in a deeply Protestant theological context and educated in Protestant institutions of higher learning. To read these works, and Anderson in particular, highlights my own sense of ambivalence – even identity crisis – in relation to that interpretive tradition. Anderson's explicitly Protestant theological return to Esther is haunted in many ways by the Holocaust, and so is my reading. Anderson is a Presbyterian professor and scholar of religion at a Presbyterian institution, and so am I. Anderson's article is steeped in the neo-orthodox theological tradition of the 1930s and 1940s, and my own theological education at Columbia Theological Seminary (a Presbyterian seminary related to Anderson's) was likewise pervaded by this tradition. In fact, Anderson's textbook, *Understanding the Old Testament* (1986), was my first introduction to the Hebrew

11

Bible during my first semester at Columbia. Anderson's interpretation represents some of the most conscientious work done on Esther
within my own Protestant interpretive tradition, and yet I have come
to find it terribly problematic, dependent on a logic of sameness
that cannot escape the self/not-self opposition. Reading this work
closely in the present context is necessarily a self-critical activity,
which sharpens my own experience of dislocation. It is closest, and
most alien.

Throughout the interpretive tradition I have sketched here, Esther
appears as the remotest Jewish outpost in the Christian Old Testament. As such it has a knack for flushing out representations of the
Jew as other. Not entirely successful at revising this interpretive
tradition, moreover, Anderson's interpretation highlights a latent
ambivalence in these representations of the Jew as the *other within* –
simultaneously necessary and excluded, compelling and repulsive,
the source and degeneration of revelation, self and other. Christian
identity, like modern Western European identity in general, has
tended to depend on the Jew even while defining itself over against
the Jew. Such ambivalences are a hallmark of colonialism, as Bhabha
and others have shown. As one attends to them, common assumptions about otherness and identity become profoundly problematic,
and one begins to realize that, in order to think about the problem
of the other (the "Jewish problem," for example), one must think
seriously about the problem of the self. Although not particularly
self-reflective, Anderson's text opens a door to self-reflection on
ambivalences within the identity that is constructed over against the
Jew in the Christian colonial discourse on Jewish Scripture.

DARK CONTINENT

Simone de Beauvoir, whose *Second Sex* is roughly contemporary
with Anderson's article (the French edition was first published in
1949), has shown how a strikingly similar master/slave dynamic of
identity construction has pervaded Western androcentric discourse
on woman and the feminine as quintessentially other.

> man never thinks of himself without thinking of the Other; he
> views the world under the sign of duality, which is not in the
> first place sexual in character. But being different from man,
> who sets himself up as the same, it is naturally to the category
> of the Other that woman is consigned; the Other includes

woman. . . . When woman's role enlarges, she comes to represent almost in its entirety the region of the Other.

(1989: 69; cf. 64–5)

Within this political and epistemological frame, significantly enough,
Beauvoir argues that woman, like the Jew for many Protestant
interpreters, most often represents immanence and earthiness, whereas man represents transcendence (e.g., 1989: xxviii, 57, 248). We have
seen a strikingly similar dynamic of identity-building in Protestant
interpretive discourse, where the Jew most often represents immman-
ence and earthiness and the Christian represents transcendence.
Indeed, in *The Second Sex* Beauvoir insists on comparing the political
situation of women to that of Jews (e.g., 1989: 128).

Drawing from Beauvoir's classic analysis of this androcentric
system of representation, Hélène Cixous (1976: 885) has described
the feminine imaginary as the ultimate "dark continent" within
phallocratic logic, suggesting that it, too, depends on a kind of
colonialism. In a way similar to Christian anti-Judaism, moreover,
both Beauvoir and Cixous, among others, highlight the vulnerabilities and ambivalences of the (masculine) self that takes form over
against the other woman.

This parallel between the two discourses (on the Jew as other and
the woman as other) is certainly evident in Esther where, as my
reading shows, there are many convergences between projections of
the other woman and the other Jew, as well as between the two
subjects who project these two others and mark them for oblivion
as such. In Esther, as we shall see, sexual politics is ethnic politics is
national politics. Representations of the other in terms of gender are
inextricably linked to constructions of the other in terms of ethnicity.
My engagements with feminist theory throughout this book will
"orient" my reading of Esther toward thinking the limits of *both*
ethnic and gender identity. This theoretical discourse can be difficult
going for some readers who are not accustomed to it. But it is worth
the extra effort at understanding, because it allows us to focus not
only on how self and other are defined – whether in terms of gender
or ethnicity – but also on the ways those definitions are always
unstable and open to dislocation and sabotage.

To critique the dynamics of identity-building and projection is
not, however, to purchase a place among the colonized. It is possible,
and I believe imperative, that a subject like myself destabilize the very
identities that endow privilege at the expense of others. But to think

one can simply defect, jump over to the "other side," would be a fantasy – a fantasy that in fact depends on the very self/other opposition that needs to be rethought. On the contrary, the critique, which is a self-critique, is ultimately *unsettling*, leaving the moment of this encounter with the book of Esther in-between, identified neither with the projected other (Vashti, Esther, Mordecai, the Jews) who overlives nor with the self (Memucan, Haman, the king) whose sense of stability and location is deconstructed in the process of that overliving. This book must begin in dislocation, and can advance only by traversing thresholds, by an exegesis that traces hauntings to deeper and deeper levels of dislocation. Esther is a writing in diaspora, about identity in dispersion and under threat. It plays between annihilation and Purimfest, between desert and carnival. To read it honestly, self-reflectively, demands that I too find myself on the edge of the desert, haunted by echoes of carnival.

The moment of this reading is indeed haunted – haunted by presences that remain unrepresentable, haunted by pains and losses that present themselves as gaps, as absences, as echoes of echoes of muffled screams, even as unspeakable, unwriteable ovens. These hauntings will obligate. Thus the moment of this reading is also necessarily an *ethical moment*, for the realization of the presence of a haunting is like a confrontation with the face of the other, an "ultimate situation," as Emmanuel Levinas puts it. "The face remains present in its refusal to be contained" (Levinas 1969: 81). Naked and hungry, transitory, transient, even spectral, it calls forth a shudder of thought. Likewise the presence of a haunting. It must be allowed to enter consciousness and to disturb, even judge, without being integrated, subsumed, coopted, contained. To try to *make sense* of it, to fix it in a web of meaning, to *speak for* it, is to lose it again even while fooling oneself into thinking one has been accountable – has *given account* – and thereby has located oneself and one's reading. One can only give account to the presence of a haunting by acknowledging debt, lack, delinquency. It is always too little, too late. Yet nonetheless necessary. This is not the book I thought I was writing. But it is the book that I needed to write.

1

WRITING OUT, I

Then, in the presence of the king and the officials, Memucan said, "Queen Vashti has transgressed not only against the king, but also against all the chiefs, and against all the people in every one of King Ahasuerus's provinces. For word of the queen will go out to all the women, and they will despise their lords with their eyes, saying 'King Ahasuerus said to bring Vashti the queen into his presence, and she did not come.' On that day the women of the chiefs of Persia-Media will talk to the chiefs of the king concerning the word that they heard about the queen, and there will be plenty of contempt and wrath. If it pleases the king, let a royal word go out from his presence, and let it be written among the laws of the Persians and the Medes so that it may not be changed, that Vashti shall never again come into the presence of King Ahasuerus, and let the king give her royal status to another who is more pleasing than her. Thus when the decree of the king is heard thoughout all his kingdom – vast as it is – all women will give rightful honor to their lords, from the greatest to the least."

(Est 1:16–20)

Unroll the scroll of Esther, and open onto a many-splendored sea of booze. Indeed, it often appears that drinking parties are what float the plot. In the first nine verses of the story alone, there are three drinking parties. The first two are hosted by King Ahasuerus, who, as the story progresses, turns out to be a real wino who never turns down a drinking party. The third is hosted by Queen Vashti, very soon to be *ex*-Queen Vashti, written out by royal law for her refusal to be the king's favorite object. Indeed, as the story opens, and as the wine flows from on high – and as the king becomes quite full of it – one quickly realizes that, in this kingdom, parties have something to do with national politics, and that national politics has something to do with sexual politics.

15

OPENINGS

When I ask college students in introductory biblical studies courses to give a synopsis of the book of Esther, I often find that the story of Vashti in chapter 1 is left out entirely. Why? Certainly it is not due to a lack of interest in this opening story, for once I ask them about Vashti we often spend the rest of the class session discussing her story and the sexual-political issues it raises. Rather, I suspect that many simply do not know what to do with it in relation to the rest of the book. How does this story about a woman who refuses to be the object of the king's all-male gang ogle relate to the story of the orphan Jewish queen of Persia, her cousin Mordecai, and the struggle against Haman and his plans to annihilate all Jews? What kind of an "opening" is this?

Without realizing it, most of my students are dealing with this question much as a formalist biblical scholar would. They are reading chapter 1 as a story that serves its function within the larger narrative and then disappears nearly without a trace; that is, this opening is understood to be making space in the royal court for the entry of the permanent ("real") cast members, after which it erases most of itself (except, of course, the king) and the questions it raises before they arrive. And so when it becomes time to talk about the story of Esther, Vashti gets short shrift.

Suspecting that there may be more to this opening in relation to the narrative that follows, my reading avoids such formal de-capitation. As a way into the story world of Esther, I will argue that the gender-based conflict which opens the narrative indicates, on the one hand, the vulnerability of the "patriarchy" it is presenting, and, on the other, the extremes to which the male subject will go in order to maintain his position over against the woman-as-object. At the same time, the text locates dynamics of gender identity-building within a larger apparatus of ethnic identity-building. In the process of opening the story, then, Esther 1 opens up the possibility of a critique of the very gender- and ethnicity-coded political order it introduces.

Moreover, insofar as the narrative, in farcical fashion, indicates vulnerabilities within this kind of patriarchy, it also, more generally, insinuates the vulnerability of ostensible, centralized consolidations of power to peripheral subversion. As it makes a farce of royal, masculine power relations, it encourages identifications with that royal power's ultimate *abject*, that which is neither subject nor object within the present order and which must therefore be pushed outside its borders. The abject is "what disturbs identity, system, order. What does not respect borders, positions, rules" (Kristeva 1982: 4; see below). In this case abjection is embodied in the other woman who refuses to be reduced to the object of the male ogle; later it will be embodied in the other Jew, construed as Persian law's quint-essential perversion. As will be seen in subsequent chapters, the text of Esther builds a striking solidarity between the other woman Vashti, marked over against the subjects of the law (the king, Memucan, and the other officials), and *Mordecai* as the "other Jew" over against the same (but with Haman replacing Memucan). Thus as we read we may identify not with the subject of the law, at the center of ostensible power, but with the one marked for oblivion as that subject's antithesis, and with forms of covert power that rely primarily on ambiguity.

HONOR, PLEASURE, AND OTHER DIFFICULT OBJECTIVES

After a brief sketch of the setting (vv. 1–3a), the text dives straight into the first two drinking parties, hosted by the primary subject, King Ahasuerus (vv. 3b–8).[1] The fact that drinking is the primary focus of these festivals is clear not only from the word designating them (*mishteh*, a noun form of the Hebrew verb "to drink"), but also from the details describing them. Other than the decor in verse 6, all the details given about the parties have to do with drinking: the goblets in which the drinks were given, the potency of the wine, and the kind of drinking ("without constraint") that the king wants his guests to enjoy.[2]

The first drinking fest lasts 180 days and includes all the king's high officials and nobility who are "in his presence," or more literally, "to his face" (*lᵉpanayw*).[3] The host's interest, explicitly related in verse 4, is to display his unequaled honor, greatness, and wealth. The kingdom is so secure that all its high officials can party on at the king's open bar in the palace of Susa for over half a year. When the party is over, the king directs his attention to the other strata of his royal dominion, namely, "all the people who were found in the acropolis of Susa, from greatest to least" (v. 5), which advances and extends his purpose of displaying his own greatness. Thus the second party works to exhibit his unequaled greatness and honor over every social stratum. Already, then, a picture is developing in which all ostensible power, from greatest to least, is consolidated around and identified with the king, and with the palace at Susa as its central, physical location.

One can map the space of this narrative world as it emerges in terms of concentric circles of power. The king and his officials are located in the palace as the centermost ring, and the king himself, vacuous though he may be, is in the center of that center. In the second ring is Susa, and in the third ring are all the provinces "from India to Ethiopia." Certain other details of this map will become important as the narrative develops. For example, the boundaries (palace gates, city gates, territorial borders), as threshold markers or limins, will gain significance, as will liminal figures such as Mordecai and the eunuchs who are often found occupying those thresholds.

Throughout these first eight verses, which are focused primarily on the innermost ring of power, emphasis on the security and greatness of Ahasuerus's reign is excessive.[4] There are, for example, five references to the king's rule (*m-l-k* in nominal or verbal forms). Territorial references are mentioned repeatedly, along with several other words or phrases suggesting pre-eminence and/or security ("resting securely," v. 2; "glorious" or "weighty riches," "honor," "splendor of his greatness," "numerous," v. 4; high numbers, vv. 1, 4–5; and lavish descriptions of the party decor, vv. 6–7). Perhaps most significantly, the purpose of the festivals is explicitly aimed at demonstrating the king's *honor* (v. 4). Indeed, honor, most closely associated in Esther with *yᵉqar*, is a central theme throughout the entire narrative, and emerges already here as an important means for consolidating power.[5] As will soon become clear, moreover, the king's royal honor, as presented here, is not unrelated to every man's honor, especially concerning their status over against women. Such excessive emphasis on the king's power pushes, it would seem, any insecurities to the margins. On the other hand, margins will possess no small significance in Esther.

The language of *proximity* in this narrative, already prevalent in the opening eight verses, also deserves special notice, for through it the relations between spatial location, identity, and power emerge as particularly significant. The phrase "in the presence of" (the construct *lipnê* or something closely related) occurs nine times in chapter 1 alone, all in reference to the king. In each case, it carries a connotation of control: to be in the king's presence is – at least ostensibly – to be under his control. The hierarchical social order, on top of which the king "rests securely" (v. 2), can only be maintained if other members of that order remain fully present – or at least as long as they are readily presentable. This necessity will be especially important when it comes to Vashti.

In addition to proximity/distance – which itself implies inside/ outside as well – the narrative is dominated by the discourse of pleasing/displeasing, which is developed primarily through verbal and adjectival forms of the word *tob* ("good," "pleasing," "to be good," "to be pleasing"), and which is especially prevalent at key junctures in the narrative action involving the king. For example, it occurs five times in the interchanges of 1:10–22, with four of those occurrences concentrated around Vashti's refusal to come and her subsequent ban (vv. 11, 19 [twice], and 21; see the subsequent discussion). To "be pleasing" is to confirm, or at least to *appear* to confirm, the order of things, to maintain stasis. Within the sexual political order, beauty and pleasure are associated with objecti- fication – to be one of the objects by which the subject secures power publicly. Insofar as objectification is associated with presentability, moreover, the integration of proximity/distance and pleasing/dis- pleasing as codes for locating ostensible power becomes particularly important. For Vashti in particular, to be pleasing will mean to remain accessible and presentable as object for the pleased male ogle.

One might well suspect, by the way, that although "from greatest to least" (v. 5) covers the social-class gamut, it may not include women. Indeed, that suspicion is confirmed in v. 9: "Also, Queen Vashti threw a drinking fest [for the] women of the royal house of King Ahasuerus." In the otherwise all-male series of events described thus far, Vashti's party stands out, both literally and figuratively. That is, it takes place elsewhere and is thrown by the other sex. Contrasted against the descriptions of the two previous festivals, moreover, the details given about this one are scant. Yet this verse is freighted with significance. It is introduced with the particle *gam* ("also"), which has the rhetorical force within the narrative of emphasizing a turn in the story while maintaining an association with the previous material. As such, this particle draws attention to a new acting subject. Up to this point, every active verb has had the king as its subject. He has "displayed" his honor, "ordered" his officials, and (twice) "thrown" or "made/prepared" (*'asah*) drinking fests. Now, it is Queen Vashti who is the acting subject. Moreover, she acts in precisely the same way the king has acted: she "throws a drinking fest" (*'astah mishteh*).

While these women are in the king's house (v. 9b), they are not

19

fully in his presence. Neither totally outside nor totally inside, both inside and outside, they are not totally in his control. Yet since they are not entirely outside, they cannot simply be dismissed as beyond his concern either. How to exclude without losing control? (A kingly dilemma indeed.) What might they be doing? Well, drinking, for one. What might they be talking about? With particular insight, and perhaps pushing the parody of male anxiety which will be particularly evident later in the chapter, Targum Sheni, an early Aramaic renarration of Esther, suggests that during her party Vashti brings the women into the king's most intimate quarters (his bedroom) and answers all their questions about his private life.[6]

Even at this early point in the narrative, then, locations of ambiguity and peripheral power begin to appear within the space of the story world – even, and perhaps most significantly, within the palace walls, within the innermost circle, at the very center of royal power.

SETTLING DIFFERENCES

On the last day of the king's second drinking party, whether out of insecurity or a desire to show off to the other men or some combination thereof, the drunken king wants to *present* Vashti to his companions. He asks his seven eunuchs to bring Vashti the queen "into the presence of" (*lipnê*) the king. While there may be some other more ritualistic aspect to this bidding that is lost to us (see Fox 1991b: 20), the text does give one explicit motive: "to display to the people and the chiefs her beauty, for she was pleasing [*tob*] to look at" (v. 11). Just as he was displaying (*beʰarʾotô . . . ʾet*) his honor and unequaled greatness in verse 4, so now he intends to display (*leʰarʾot . . . ʾet*; nearly identical wording) his queen's good looks. Given this close parallel, it is reasonable to understand the king's request here as another public display aimed at consolidating and securing power, this time by securing his subject position as the true patriarch and absolute center of it all. For the king, the narrative parallel suggests, maintenance of male subjective power in the royal household economy (*oikonomia*, "house-order") is integrally related to the maintenance of power in the larger order of things.

In all this, Vashti is treated exclusively as an object of exchange between men: she is to be brought by the eunuchs and looked upon by the king and the other men for pleasure. She is a means to identification between the king and the other men, bringing them closer together and providing their subjective position in the center with ever greater definition. They require her as the object obliged to enable their identification with one another.[7]

The king sends the eunuchs across to the women's party, in order to carry his desire to Vashti and to carry Vashti back to him. The fact that seven eunuchs are sent for her on the seventh day, moreover, may suggest that this will be the impressive finale of the king's display (the ultimate act of hospitable exchange), and that it will conclusively establish his secure resting-place on the throne.

The queen's response, however, undermines any such desire (v. 12a). In fact, her refusal to come at the king's bidding marks the first and only point in the narrative where the royal impetus is, so to speak, brought low. Just when his 187-day long demonstration of honor and power is about to come to its final climax, the party is cut short. The pleasure of an appropriate finish is frustrated, and the queen's refusal is met with burning rage.

At this point, the utter dependence of this narrative's primary male subject on her rapidly becomes clear. Ironically, however, it is not Vashti's *presence* that makes clear the royal subject's dependence on her, as well as the related dependence of the other male subjects on other women. For, as has been noted already, she is never really fully present in the narrative. Rather, it is her willful *absence*, her refusal to come, that throws a wrench into the machinery and leads to her dishonorable discharge. So long as she can be construed to be *absent by exclusion*, there is no problem. Eventually, however, the male subject requires a special object, a quintessential something to bounce off in order to remind him of how solid he is, a negative image, something to reflect his own self-made image back at him ("who's the potentest of them all?"). Of course, this dynamic reveals the male subject's special and highly problematic dependence on her as fixed object. She is the grounding for his own identity, the subject's object. From verse 10 onward, Vashti is clearly the king's primary objective, and it is equally clear from the parallel "display" of his splendor and glory in verse 4, discussed earlier, that her objective status is linked to his subjective status. Needless to say, then, her refusal to come and be pleasing to look at does not reflect well on him.

The king turns to those "wisemen" who are already "in his presence." The text emphasizes their close proximity to the king: they are "near him," they "look upon the king's face," and they are the ones "who sit first in his kingdom." These men are *not* marginal.

They are inside and up close. They are, moreover (or better, therefore), expert advisors in law and judgment, who "know the times" (*ha'ittim*, v. 13), that is, they know what is appropriate and when. The king asks (v. 15), "According to the law, what ought to be done with Queen Vashti on account of her not doing what the king told her to do by way of the eunuchs?" Vashti's refusal is experienced by the king as a disturbance in the system of relations that puts the king securely as the center of royal, masculine power. As such, it calls for a strategy of official, state-ordered response that can block the disturbing effects of her refusal and prevent it from happening again.

Memucan provides a strategy that can do that and then some. Here one finds the strongest expression of anxiety and vulnerability among the men in the story with regard to their own subjective status over against women. Interpreters have rightly noted the ridiculous panic expressed in Memucan's speech (e.g., Fox 1991b: 21–2; Moore 1971: 14; and Radday 1990: 297–8). Indeed, this is a farce. Even as the Persian lord's nightmare-vision is told, its dreamers appear as overreacting buffoons.

Memucan speaks "in the presence of [*lipnê*] the king and the officials" (v. 16),[8] projecting the broadest ramifications of the queen's transgression: "Queen Vashti has transgressed not only against the king, but also against all the chiefs, and against all the people in every one of King Ahasuerus's provinces." Like a pebble dropped in a puddle, the queen's offense is first against the king, but moves out "against all the chiefs," reverberating through every concentric ring of power, ultimately threatening the entire sexual-political order. Male fixation on/of her is crucial.

Memucan then goes on in verses 17–18 to describe what could happen when news of the queen's transgression gets out "to all the women" (*'al-kol-hannashim*; note the parallel with "all the chiefs," *'al-kol-hassarim*, in v. 16). He appears most concerned, however, with his own particular social location, for the scene quickly moves to the insurrectional words and actions of the "women of the chiefs of Persia-Media" (v. 18).

> For word of the queen will go out to all the women, and they will despise their lords with their eyes, saying "King Ahasuerus said to bring Vashti the queen into his presence, and she did not come." On that day the women of the chiefs of Persia-Media will talk to the chiefs of the king concerning the word

that they heard about the queen, and there will be plenty of contempt and wrath.

In this envisioning of the avalanche Queen Vashti has started, Memucan describes two instances in which there will be contempt ("despise . . . with their eyes" and "there will be plenty of contempt and wrath")[9] – even imagining their own counter-gaze – and two instances in which the women will "talk" (forms of the verb *'amar*). The sequence is contempt–talk–talk–contempt. At the heart of this sequence one finds two male nightmare-fantasies of women speaking. Thus far in the narrative, no one but the king and Memucan have spoken (*'amar*; vv. 10, 13, and 16). Women have had no voice – not even Vashti. Ironically, it is at the center of Mèmucan's speech, which is intended to reassert the proper deferential position of women, that male anxiety about their power to speak finds a way into the discourse.

WRITING WITH AN ERASURE

Memucan concludes, in verses 19–20, with a recommendation. He proposes that the word that will get out concerning the queen's transgression be closely followed by a "royal [written] word" that "will go out from his [the king's] presence" (*yetse' d^ebar-malkût mill^epanayw*). Thus the spoken word that could undo the order of things as Memucan envisions it must be followed by a written word that would wipe out the threat and, quite literally, reinscribe that order. It is a reinscription by erasure.

The content of the recommendation is as follows. First, Vashti (no longer referred to as "Vashti *the queen*") shall never again "come into the presence of King Ahasuerus" – ironic, since Vashti had refused to come into his presence in the first place (1:12). Moreover, her status shall be given to another who is "more pleasing" (*hattobah*) than her. Earlier I noted the integration of the codes of proximity/distance and pleasing/displeasing as a means of associating the other woman's *objectification* with her *presentability*. Thus, to be a pleasing object for the male subject, the woman must be readily presentable. At this point in the text, in the wake of Vashti's refusal to come into the king's presence to be the object of the pleased male ogle, Memucan recommends an undoing of Vashti using the same code: she will never again be *present*, and someone more *pleasing* (presentable, objectifiable) will fill the space left by her.

Vashti has become, quite literally, *abject*: she can be neither subject nor object within the social and symbolic order, and therefore she must be repulsed, pushed outside its boundaries. Up to the point of her refusal, her place was ambivalent. As already observed, she was neither totally inside nor totally outside (i.e., her party took place elsewhere, but nonetheless in the palace "that was King Ahasuerus's"). She threw, furthermore, a party just as the king did, and the narrative uses identical language to describe the actions of both subjects (vv. 3, 5, and 9). She was more than – or rather *other than* – an object. Within the world of the narrative, then, the king's demand that she be brought into his presence and be the good-looking object of the male ogle aimed to settle and reduce that ambivalence and excess once and for all – to pin things down, and thereby to secure the king's own identity. Refusing to come and be looked at, thereby rejecting the status of fixed object (perhaps finding it objectionable, as Targum Sheni suggests), and being refused the status of full subject, she must be banished, abjected.[10] Oblivion will be her "place."

Memucan concludes by describing what will happen when news of this decree concerning Vashti is disseminated (v. 20). Put simply, the disastrous scenario imagined in verses 17–18 will be reversed. Women will once again "give rightful honor to their lords" – the same honor (y^eqar) that the king has been eager to display since the beginning of the story (v. 4).

As with the interchange between the king and Vashti (vv. 10–12), this second interchange concludes in verses 21–2 with the king's reaction: his "pleasure" returns (*wayîtab*). Whereas Vashti left the king undone, Memucan does him good. Royal dispatches are sent throughout the kingdom. The proper order of things – a proper grammar, getting all its subjects and objects straight – is rewritten throughout every territory. Boundaries are re-marked and re-enforced. And the message is universally the same, no matter what language or what script is used to communicate it: every man will "act as chief" (*sorer*) in his household, "from greatest to least." As above, so below.

Fox (1991b: 209) rightly comments that Memucan's speech here is both a clear presentation and powerful legal enforcement of the sexual politics that grounds male identity within the king's order. Ironically, Vashti's refusal to become an object of exchange between the king and the other men has led to another kind of "use" for her within the sexual politics delineated by Memucan. That is, she has become, by force, an object lesson for other women throughout the king's dominion, to keep their places within the household economy.

Vashti has been written out (beyond the bounds of both the law and the story). There is indeed a kind of writing that erases. Writing is "writing in," literally *in-scription*, but it can also be "writing out," or, as Jean-Luc Nancy puts it in *The Birth to Presence* (1993: 333–40), *exscription*. Writing is *é[x]criture*, an act of *writing in* that is also an act of *writing out*. In the context of Nancy's discourse, the term refers primarily to writing as a process of exscribing "existence itself," or the "real" (in Georges Bataille's sense; see, e.g., 1989: 27–32), which in itself is not representable, but which is present only in its being "extracted" into the book. Thus the act of inscribing into the book is always an act of sacrifice – a giving-over, a dedication, a marking-off – and in this sense is exscription. In the present context, I am referring more narrowly to the act of exscribing the other woman (who is unrepresentable, unfixable within the male sexual economy) in the process of reinscribing a particular sexual-political law. This act on the part of Memucan and the king is, in this sense, a *reinscription by exscription*: Vashti is *written out* of both the law and the story, and this writing-out is used by the subjects of the law to *write back in* what they consider to be proper sexual identity for women in relation to "their lords" (even though it may have never existed before this).[11]

The book of Esther suggests a further ironic dimension to this process of exscription. Exscription serves to mark territory by naming that which belongs outside it; yet precisely in this process of marking off for oblivion, Vashti and her refusal are also indelibly *written into* the story in a way that will be difficult to forget. To mark off, to abject by written law, the woman who refuses to be a pleasing object of male exchange, is also to draw attention to her and even to acknowledge the threat to male domination she represents. Thus this text demonstrates the ironic impossibility of marking for oblivion – of the one (the identical) enforcing political amnesia with regard to the other. Chapter 1 remains in memory of her, traced with the spectral presence-by-absence of this other woman.

VASHTI'S SURVIVAL

The next brief passage (2:1–4), which stands between the story of Vashti's being written out and the story of Esther's being signed in, marks the passage between two queens. It is the passageway from

Queen Vashti to Queen Esther. In this sense it marks the crossing of a threshold, a sur-vival (over-living or passing beyond). It is actually a double survival: it marks Esther's survival of Vashti, as well as Vashti's own survival – or at least the survival of her trace-memory – into the narrative that follows.

With Vashti written out by royal decree, we find ourselves left in the company of Persian fools, at the center of whom is a dangerous power vacuum called the king. The eye lingers, perhaps even mourns, over the blank space left by Vashti.[12] Who can fill the space left by this erased other woman?

Apparently the king, too, is unable to forget her. Julia Kristeva's words about abjection are suggestive with regard to Vashti's abjection: as the story leaves her behind, she remains as "the *land of oblivion* that is constantly remembered. Once upon blotted-out time, the abject must have been a magnetized pole of covetousness" (1982: 8). Vashti had refused to be brought in as a pleasing-to-look-at object among men; now, in Est 2:1–4, it is the *memory of that refusal* that makes it impossible for the king to forget her. In this sense, it is actually Vashti's resistance to being forgotten, rather than the lack of a queen, that motivates the pageant-search for her replacement.

Verses 1–4 are patterned like the second half of chapter 1 (1:12–21): the king is displeased (2:1; cf. 1:12); a recommendation is made that will rectify the problem (2:2–4a; cf. 1:16–20); "and the word was pleasing in the king's eyes, and he did thus" (2:4b; cf. 1:21).[13]

Est 2:1 begins by delineating this episode from the previous one in terms of time: "*After these things, when* King Ahasuerus's rage had settled down. . ." Yet it also serves to link what follows to what has preceded. This is accomplished primarily by the phrase "after these things." It is more specifically linked to the sexual-political conflict by mention of the king's "rage" (*hamah*) which he felt in reaction to Vashti's refusal. The overall parallel of 2:1–4 with 1:12–21 further develops this connection. Thus Vashti persists as the problem. "After these things, when King Ahasuerus's rage had settled down, he remembered Vashti and what she did, and what was decreed against her" (2:1). Precisely what did the king remember of Vashti? Susan Niditch (1987: 133–4) suggests that this verse includes "an erotic suggestion. 'The king remembered what Vashti used to do' (2:1), presumably 'for him.' He does not miss a person or a personality but a function." Yet to read it as such is to disregard the previous trauma of Vashti's refusal and banishment, which is both implicitly and explicitly referenced in this verse. First, the phrase "what she did" (*'et 'asher-'asatah*) alludes to her refusal to come, as summarized in the king's request for legal advice (1:15): "According to the law, what ought to be done with Queen Vashti on account of her not doing [*'asher lo'-'astah*] what [*'et*] the king told her?" Second, in order to read it as Niditch does, one must ignore the other half of what the king remembers, that is, the decree for her banishment. The king remembers the conflict. In this sense, Vashti's initial refusal becomes her refusal to be forgotten by the king as well. In both cases, the king's pleasure is deferred.

The verb used to describe Vashti's official exscription from the story (a Niphal perfect form of *gazar*) is of particular significance. In most cases where this verb is used in reference to "cutting off" (e.g., Habakkuk 3:17; 2 Chronicles 26:21; Psalm 88:6), it occurs with the preposition "from" (*min*; but cf. Isaiah 53:8). In Est 2:1, however, *'aleyah* follows the verb (thus "against her," "over her," or "concerning her"). Given the context of chapter 1, where Vashti was removed from her status as queen and from the story itself, this preposition allows the verb to indicate both the official written "decree" against her and the actual "cutting-off." In this sense, *gazar* is the most literal Hebrew equivalent for *exscription*.[14]

Verses 2–4a then present the recommendation offered by the "servants of the king," whose function in the narrative is much like that of the advisors in the previous episode concerning Vashti's transgression.[15] Their recommendation – which the king will follow word-for-word, as he did Memucan's – is as follows:

> Let them seek out, for the king, young virgins, *pleasing to look at*. And let the king appoint appointees in all the provinces of his kingdom. And they will gather every young virgin, *pleasing to look at*, to the acropolis of Susa, to the harem [lit., house of women], into the hand of Heggai,[16] the king's eunuch, keeper of the women. And he will give them their beauty treatment. And the girl who is *pleasing in the eyes of the king* will be made queen instead of Vashti.

As already discussed, Memucan's recommendation in 1:16–20 served both to officially reinscribe the objectification of women and to remove the problem presented by Vashti's refusal of that role. Interestingly enough, this recommendation serves basically the same purpose. There is, for example, a persistent objectification of the young women. This takes place on two levels. First, syntactically, they are never the subject of verbs, but only objects; they are sought, gathered, kept, and given their preparatory beauty treatments.[17] In all this, they are exchanged among, or passed between, men (from their father's house to the king's). (Note, too, that here again, as in 1:10, the primary mediator between the women and the king will be a eunuch.) Second, visually, their status as good-looking objects of the pleased male ogle is emphasized, almost to the point of excess: they are described as "pleasing to look at" (*tôbat mar'eh*) twice; they will be given "beauty treatments" by Heggai; and the one "pleasing in the eyes of the king" will be given the highest regard, by being made queen. Indeed, passive looks appear to be the only criterion.

In all this, moreover, there is a strong recollection of Vashti – in terms of both *identification with* and *contrast over against*. Vashti, too, was described as "pleasing to look at" (*tôbat mar'eh*; 1:11), and the king at least attempted to objectify her as a commodity to be brought in and shared with other men. In contrast to Vashti, however, these women will be sought, brought, and kept without resistance. It is explicitly stated, moreover, that the one most pleasing will be made queen *"instead of [tahat] Vashti"* (2:4a), as Memucan had proposed, nearly word-for-word. Thus the advice readily acknowledges, on the one hand, that the replacement must be like Vashti (i.e., "pleasing to look at"), and yet, on the other, that it is the memory of Vashti's *refusal* – indeed, it is the *refusal itself* – that must be overcome. The first action, recommended by Memucan in 1:16–20, apparently was not enough, was not total in its removal of the problem. Vashti and her transgression were written out by writing in a new, irrevocable law, erased in permanent marker. But erasure marks remain: Vashti remains.

28

2

PALIMPSEST

Think of the book of Esther as a kind of palimpsest: a story is written, then erased, and then a new story is written over the old, erased one. The story of the other woman is written over by the story of the other Jew. Vashti is erased, and in different ways Esther and Mordecai will each occupy the blank spaces she leaves behind. Traces of the other woman will be legible on the other Jew. Vashti will survive her own end in the narrative. She will haunt the rest of the story. The story of Esther and Mordecai never shakes her memory.

Vashti's story, then, is no simple preface to the "main body" of the book.

In an essay on Hegel's use and understanding of the preface (1981: 1–59), Jacques Derrida writes, "Prefaces, along with forewords, introductions, preludes, preliminaries, preambles, prologues, and prolegomena, have always been written, it seems, in view of their own self-effacement. Upon reaching the end of the *pre-* . . . , the route which has been covered must cancel itself out" (8). In this way, such beginnings are construed as peripheral to and distinct from the "main body" of the writing – whether that "main body" is a totalizing philosophy of the subject of history, such as Hegel's,[1] or a story about a struggle to deliver the Jews of Persia from an anti-Jewish pogrom. They cancel themselves out, erase themselves, before things "really" get started.

But that prefatory beginning can never be entirely removed by the time the "main body" of the narrative begins. A remainder (French *restance*, close to "resistance") always traces itself into the rest of the writing. The remainder resists total removal. As Derrida puts it (1981: 9), "this subtraction leaves a mark of erasure, a remainder which is added to the subsequent text and which cannot be completely summed up within it." This erasure mark implies what was erased, what was taken out – an other-than, which is not readily available or containable from the inside, but which is also never totally removed. The clear "opposition between pre-text and text" (41) is blurred.

As the reader moves out of chapter 1 and into the "main story" or "narrative proper," the beginning *leaves the mark of erasure.* This is an especially intriguing way to think about the book of Esther, which is about writing laws that aim to shore up particular identities by erasing those who are "privileged" to represent divergence or antithesis according to those laws. Derrida's reflections help articulate another dimension of the problematics of identity politics in the story: the other can never "fit" cozily with the same, for it is neither the same nor the opposite; the logic of the same will work either to reduce it (to sameness or opposition) or to erase it, but neither can be entirely successful. There will always be a trace, a remainder, an erasure mark, the sign of a departure of something that is not part of the present order of things. As remainder-left-behind-in-leaving, the trace resists (*resistance/restance*) forgetting that the order being inscribed is never total, and therefore never totally secure.

As noted earlier, it is common in studies of Esther to bracket off Vashti's story in chapter 1 from having a significant role in the subsequent story, to treat it as a kind of narrative preface that is important for setting the stage for what follows but unessential to the main body of the narrative. The story of the other woman is quickly forgotten as the reader moves into the story of the other Jew. One reason for this bracketing is that, although biblical scholarship often focuses on either ethnic identity or gender identity, it rarely considers these two identity codes in relation to one another. Thus the story of the attempted exscription of the other woman (by Memucan and the king) in chapter 1 seems to have little or no relation to the attempted exscription of the other Jew (by Haman and the king) in subsequent chapters. Strong narrative parallels, I will argue, suggest otherwise.

Formal and structural strategies of literary analysis also have encouraged readers to sever Vashti from the main body of the narrative. The king's question in Est 1:15 is also often the biblical critic's question: "According to the law, what ought to be done with Queen Vashti?" That is, what, from the perspective of a formal analysis of the book of Esther as a whole, ought to be done with this opening story? Indeed, there are exegetical "laws" and methodological regulations according to which such decisions must be made. In scholarship on Esther, many of these laws go back to turn-of-the-century formalist assumptions. Such assumptions maintain particular functions or roles for certain characters according to particular narrative types. As a result, the characters in a story (especially "less developed" ones) are perceived in such a way that their identities remain discrete from one another, insofar as each serves a particular purpose in the advancement of the plot. Thus characters do not overlap. Characters are largely reduced to identification with particular types in world literature (e.g., Vashti might be indexed as a "banished queen"; Esther might be a Cinderella type), thereby reducing the possibility of overlap or convergence. The same holds true for the overall narrative's particular sub-narratives, which are understood to serve singular functions and then are to be left behind once that function is accomplished.

The structural approach that understands Esther in terms of a system or pattern of plot reversals also finds no way to make sense of the opening story of Vashti.[2] Indeed, given that most of the story's characters disappear by chapter 2, it seems "natural" to understand this opening as peripheral to the conflict driving the "main" plot line and establishing its "basic" structure; that is, the first chapter draws the reader into the story world, introduces the king and his ingratiatingly festive persuasions, makes a space in the royal court for Esther, and then erases most of itself before the "real" story begins. Vashti is simply a border personality and has little to do with the main body of Esther.

But erasure marks remain on the surfaces that cannot necessarily be perceived in terms of such formal or structural patterning. The book of Esther not only admits this fact but exploits it. I have shown how Vashti's refusal to come and be shared as a good-looking object among the other men was taken as a threat to the male subject's status. Memucan makes this sexual politics explicit (1:16–20), but his proposal also performs another task. Without its legal implementation, Vashti would have remained other without being reduced to oppositional object – without "reflecting well." Memucan provides a means of commodifying and using her in another way, other than as object: if she will not be object, she will be written out as *abject* (abject: throw out). Resisting objectification and being refused subjectivity, she is marked by law for the land of oblivion, the land of outlaws. If she will not be objectified, then she will be *ab*jectified. Thus, ironically, by her exscription, she becomes an *object lesson* for other women (1:20). She – or rather, written word of her (her representa-

31

tion within the legal-political discourse) – is used to reinscribe and to underline the binary oppositional order of sexual politics in the story.

Yet, insofar as her *exscription* is a reinscription of the law, it is also an *inscription* of her transgression, thereby enforcing memory of her as threat. As a result, her exscription exposes insecurities in the sexual-political order being presented and opens that order to its own deconstruction. Esther's opening, the story of the other woman Vashti's exscription, makes a farce of the royal power it introduces, especially the king's and Memucan's consolidation of power in terms of sexual identity. As a way into the narrative of Esther as a whole, the story of the other woman's exscription opens to critical reflection on the problematics of identity-coded politics and the possibilities of political subversion and transformation introduced by those problematics. It is a mistake to treat Vashti's story as peripheral or pretextual to what follows in chapters 2–10, to which I now turn. The line often drawn between this narrative beginning about the other woman and the "main body" of the narrative, ostensibly about the other Jew, is not so clear. There is a great deal of spill-over. To pretend that this narrative beginning, as a sort of pretext or frame, has erased itself in order to make way for the "real story" would be, ironically, very much akin to pretending with the king and Memucan that their exscription of the other woman had likewise removed all doubts about the security of their sexual politics. As the narrative moves into questions concerning Jewish identity, traces of the other woman and her refusal will survive, living beyond the story of her exscription in chapter 1, and further compounding the problematics of political strategies based on projections of either the other Jew or the other woman. They cannot be separated.

MAIN BODY

Suddenly, as the king resolves to find someone to replace Vashti, or rather to supercede her, the narrative makes a sharp turn away from the court discussion involving the king and his advisors, and toward two Jews, Mordecai and Esther (2:5). In fact, it appears to be not so much a turn as a new legendary beginning, looping back to chapter 1, verse 1. Like a palimpsest, however, this new beginning is written over the old, and we must wonder how far we actually are from that other story.

"A Jewish man there was in the acropolis of Susa, and his name

was Mordecai ben Yair ben Shimei ben Qish, a Benjaminite man, . . ."
(2:5).[3] Even in these initial few words about the first Jew to be
introduced in the narrative, there are allusions to other biblical texts
that add both *depth* and *intertextual static* to Mordecai's Jewish
identity. Mordecai is a Benjaminite, like the ousted King Saul, and,
especially through association with the name Shimei, this is a negative
marker *within* the Judean order aligned with King David. In 2 Samuel
16, precisely as David is going into exile, his house crumbling all
around him, he encounters opposition from a Benjaminite named
Shimei (2 Samuel 16:5–14), a voice from Saul's former regime. In that
story, the location of Shimei and the tribe of Benjamin in relation to
David and the centralized Judahite monarchy is both marginal and
subversive: David encounters him on the margins of his kingdom,
on his way into exile, and Shimei introduces the most harsh, curse-
ridden criticism of David to appear anywhere in the books of Samuel.
Indeed, David later charges Solomon to "bring his gray head down
to Sheol" (2 Kings 2:9). Benjamin, moreover, is a sort of in-between
tribe in biblical literature. Is it Judahite (the name of the southern
kingdom) or Israelite (northern kingdom)? It is assumed to be
northern but seems to be traded off to the southern kingdom. Does
Judean identity ultimately, after the fall of both kingdoms, become
synonymous with Jewish identity? Does "Judean" equal "Jewish"?
If so, what is a "Benjaminite"? Mordecai is introduced as a Ben-
jaminite and a "Jew," or more precisely a Judean ($y^e h\hat{u}d\hat{\imath}$, related to
Judah, $y^e h\hat{u}dah$), with further allusions (via the story of Shimei) that
identify him with insurrection against the Davidic line. Already,
then, at this initial introduction of the first Jewish character in the
narrative, his very title suggests ambiguity in Jewish identity.

All other details that develop Mordecai's Jewish identity are
concentrated on the trauma of *exile*. Indeed, exile is explicitly
mentioned four times in verse 6 alone: he was "*exiled* from Jerusalem
with the *exiles* who were *exiled* with Jeconiah king of Judah, whom
Nebuchadnezzar king of Babylon had *exiled*."[4] To be Jewish is, in
the book of Esther, to know exile as a formative experience. To be a
Jew, after 587 BCE, is always to have been unhomed. Jewish identity
in Esther is always already dispersed, dislocated.

Thus Mordecai's Jewish character is here associated with (1) a
disenfranchised genealogy, including an ousted dynasty and a raving
anti-Davidean executed as a political criminal, and (2) exile, the
experience of being carried off and dispersed. These are the two
points in biblical historiography by which the Jewish man Mordecai

is "identified." In all this, moreover, the text encourages an identi-fication of the biblical reader with him, insofar as he is the only Jew thus far introduced in the story, and insofar as his character is filled out with "insider" details, the full significance of which is grasped only in relation to other biblical texts and knowledge of Jewish history.

Yet there is one other element of Mordecai's identity mentioned: the young woman Esther. Esther is introduced first in terms of her relation to Mordecai, as an aspect of Mordecai, an object of his "taking" and "fostering":[5]

> And it happened that he was fostering Hadassah,[6] that is, Esther, daughter of his uncle, for there was no father or mother for her. And the young woman was beautiful in form, and was pleasing to look at. And when her father and mother died, Mordecai took her for himself, as his own daughter.
>
> (2:7)

The structure of this verse is suggestive. It begins and ends with Mordecai acting on Esther (his cousin) in a way that identifies her under his super-vision: he "fosters" and "takes [*laqah*] as daughter." Between these two actions the text offers two crucial pieces of information: (1) both her mother and father have died; and (2) she is "beautiful in form" (*yᵉpat-to'ar*) and "pleasing to look at" (*tôbat mar'eh*). Indeed, this information is patterned in such a way that her "good looks" are couched between the two mentions of her lack of parents. This peculiar mix of sexual attraction (especially given *yᵉpat-to'ar*[7]) and lack of family makes Mordecai's motivations for taking her at best ambiguous. Esther would have been a permitted marriage for Mordecai, and the text appears as if it leans in that direction – until we come to the phrase "as daughter."

In relation to the preceding context, furthermore, this verse establishes both identification *with* and contrast *against* Vashti. Vashti is the only other character described in the story as "pleasing to look at" (*tôbat mar'eh*; 1:11). By contrast, Esther, as of yet, has no status other than that of object: she has been looked upon and acted upon only. Thus she is positioned in the narrative to fill the blank Vashti left, while resolving the tension brought on by Vashti's refusal of status as object.

In a way similar to the introduction of Mordecai in verses 5–6, then, the selective details offered in verse 7 about Esther are significant, for they make clear Esther's precarious place as orphaned, exiled Jewoman within the story world, while emphasizing her potential status as object of exchange among men. In this way she finds herself signed up before beginning to play. Yet this is only the beginning of her conscription, and what follows suggests that she may be playing already, albeit in very subtle, even covert ways.

Immediately following this introduction of Mordecai and Esther in 2:5–7, the text returns to the king's project of enlisting young women in a search for Vashti's replacement. Not surprisingly, Esther is one of the enlistees. Thus Esther goes from being "taken" (*laqah*) by Mordecai to being "taken" (again *laqah*) along with the other young women into another man's (i.e., the king's) house, into the hand of Heggai, "keeper of the women." She has now been conscripted twice, into two houses, "taken" from one man's house to another. Once in this new realm, however, Esther "gains favor" or "loyalty" (*hesed*) from Heggai, so that he hastens her preparations, gives her "seven chosen young women" to serve her, and switches her up to the "best of the house of the women" (2:9).

In this series of passive constructions of Esther, what is the significance of the active verbal constructions involving her "gaining favor"? There are certainly other ways in Hebrew to phrase this in order to focus the action on Heggai's perception rather than Esther's construal of that perception. The effect here is, paradoxically, to give the object a certain subjectivity. To "gain" or, more literally, "*lift* [*nasa'*] loyalty in his eyes" is essentially to "cause him to look loyally." This is, in this sense, a play of appearances by the object, suggesting that she might possess a kind of unexpected agency in relation to the male subject – a power to lead him away from where he intends to be.[8]

Verses 10–11 return the focus momentarily to the issue of Esther's identity as Jewish cousin and daughter to Mordecai, making clear that this new identity does not overwrite the former one, but rather is added to it (in potentially problematic ways). First, in verse 10, we read that "Esther did not reveal her people, because Mordecai commanded her not to reveal." Mentioned almost as an aside here, this secret, which is hidden simply by not intentionally revealing it, will eventually become an extremely important tool for undoing a plot that would have been the end of all Persian Jews. This comment indicates, moreover, that the book of Esther does not assume that Jewish identity is readily apparent; Jewish identity does not necessarily have anything to do with looks.

Why is she commanded to hide her identity with her Jewish

people? The text offers no explanation other than that Mordecai ordered her not to reveal it. Is this identity hidden because it would discourage her rise, or even endanger her in the Persian court, as many have suggested? There is no indication that this is so, either from within the book thus far or from what can be known about Persian history generally. Is it hidden because Mordecai does not want anyone to know Esther's affiliation with him? Would (public) identification with Mordecai be (politically) disadvantageous, even dangerous? Perhaps, although again there is no indication as of yet that this is so. On the other hand, very soon there will be suggestions that both reasons may be valid, as the conflict between Haman and Mordecai comes to the fore. In any case, there is no indication at this point that this is part of some strategy *she* has in mind. It is simply another aspect of her conscription in accordance with the orders and regulations of men. It is an act of obedience to Mordecai.

The text then turns full, albeit brief, attention back to Mordecai (2:11): "Each and every day, Mordecai would walk to and fro in front of the enclosure of the house of women to learn the welfare of Esther and what was being done with her." This notice makes clear Mordecai's continued investment in Esther, that is, his concern for her personal welfare, and his investment in her for his own self-interest. These two kinds of investment will remain ambiguously entangled throughout the story. Here again, the focus is on "what was being done with her." She remains, literally, an *object of concern*. She is an object that has been exchanged between and circulated among the men and, as such, she is Mordecai's link with the central Persian politics. At the same time, Mordecai's own dependence on and investment in Esther suggests the vulnerability of his own subjective status, especially at this point in the narrative, as she moves out from under his direct control and into a new royal sphere (the inner circle) to which he has little or no access without her.

After the brief aside concerning Mordecai in 2:11, the text turns back inside the harem to describe in great detail the excesses of Persian legalism in the "beauty treatment" of the young women (2:12), which, "according to law," lasted twelve full months (six with oil of myrrh and six with perfumes). Here again, as with the legal action taken against Vashti ("According to the law, what ought to be done with Queen Vashti?" [1:15]), the term "sexual politics" takes on special significance. There is no better or more literal example of the law being written on women's bodies. In all this, moreover, the *objective* of this regulatory procedure is to prepare these women as pleasing objects for the king, so that the most pleasing one may replace Vashti, who refused that status. Butler (1990: 33) is particularly suggestive in relation to this beautification process when she writes that "Gender is the repeated stylization of the body, a set of repeated acts within a highly rigid regulatory frame that congeal over time to produce the appearance of substance."[9] These are the final touches of their engendering for a potential relation to the king.

This exaggeratedly regimented procedure does not end, however, with the selection process and beauty treatment. After the twelve months, each young woman in turn would pass over at evening from this preparatory "house of women" to the "house of the king" (2:13). The next morning she would go to the "second house of women" into the hand of another eunuch, Shaashgaz, "keeper of the concubines." She would not return to the king unless he delighted in her and called her by name. Thus, as the women cross over – or better, *are passed over* – thresholds, from one harem to the king to another harem, their object-status changes. That is, they move from "young women, pleasing to look at" to "concubines." Indeed, the fact that the king will "call by name" the one he "delights in," along with the ritualized, almost sacrificial sense of the procedure, gives Ahasuerus an almost deified character. At the same time, the excessive, "stuffed" description of the process continues the text's farce on the king and royal power.

Note too that in these crossovers and exchanges of women, the eunuchs (Heggai and Shaashgaz) again serve as mediators between the sexes. As "keepers" of the women/concubines, they provide halfway houses on the ways to and from the king. As noted earlier, the seven eunuchs in Esther 1 functioned similarly in the king's interchange with Vashti (1:10, 12, 15). In both cases the women are handled "by" or put "into the hand of" eunuchs ($b^e yad$ or $'el - yad$; 1:12, 15; 2:3, 8, 14).

This transfer process climaxes in 2:15–18, when Esther's turn arrives and she is "taken" (again the verb is *laqah*, for the third time[10]) to the king's royal house. Once again reiterating her ability to "gain favor" (here *hen* rather than *hesed*), verse 15 also notes that "she did not seek a thing, except what Heggai the keeper of the women said." By evening the king "loved Esther above all women, and she gained [both] favor [*hen*] and loyalty [*hesed*] in his presence [*l^e panayw*] above all virgins, and he placed a royal crown on her head and made her queen instead of [*tahat*] Vashti" (2:17).[11] This verse is freighted to indicate the extent to which Esther's rise is the undoing

37

of the "gender trouble" that came to the fore with Vashti. After *being taken* to his house (Vashti had refused to be brought by the eunuchs; 1:10, 12), she gains love, favor, and loyalty "in his presence" (*lᵉpanayw*; Vashti had refused to be brought "into his presence"; 1:11) above all other women, and therefore he crowns her as queen "*instead of Vashti*" (as was recommended twice; 1:19; 2:4).

This undoing of Vashti, and the return to what appears on the surface to be a resting place for royal sexual politics, is finalized by another drinking fest (2:18), as well as a holiday, including the giving of royal gifts.[12] As with the festivals in chapter 1, this royal grandiosity involves all the chiefs and civil servants as well as "all the provinces." Thus all realms of the kingdom that were touched by the trouble with Vashti are returned to the festivities.

In verses 19–20, the narrative returns briefly to Mordecai, sitting at the gate. Just as Esther is established in the centermost circle in relation to the king and royal power, this brief note pulls her back into relation to Mordecai, on the borderline (sitting at the gate), recalling his interest in the recent events. Moreover, by reiterating that Esther still had not revealed her people, "obeying Mordecai just as when she was raised by him" (v. 20), the text intensifies the pull of potentially incompatible identities on Esther. As Esther is invested in and acted upon from different directions, the injunctions on her begin to pile up: to be cousin, to be daughter, to be orphan, to be Jew, to be woman, to be pleasing, to be in exile, to be in diaspora, to be Persian queen. This aggregation of potentially incompatible identities, hidden and revealed, could well lead to the disaggregation of the royal consolidation of public power which the narrative is presenting.

The opening to the book of Esther in chapter 1 was about the other woman Vashti's exscription; this new beginning (2:5–18) is about Esther's inscription. As discussed earlier, to write out is to write in, and this writing-in is intrinsically tied to that earlier writing-out. She is signed in, at least initially, as the quintessential pleasing object of exchange between men. Thus the text reiterates her passivity and her pleasing looks on the one hand, and her ability to gain favor by strategies of appearance and concealment on the other. Here the exchange of Esther – her "circulation" – is primarily between Mordecai and the king, with two eunuchs as mediators. But it is also between the king and his population (chiefs, servants, and "all provinces"), and in this regard serves politically to re-establish and guarantee the king as ultimate potentate. The king uses her, just as

38

Vashti's exscription was used, to consolidate public power around himself.

Esther is conscripted with Vashti's breakout in mind. With her, the king and his advisors are creating their own palimpsest, looping back to the beginning of chapter 1 to write a new "love story" over the old one that had starred Vashti as supporting actress. With the drinking party in 2:18 celebrating Vashti's replacement by Esther, it is as if the king were saying, "Now, where were we?" But the old story cannot be erased entirely; it will remain legible between the lines and between the words of the new story, resisting oblivion.

3

THE BIBLE AS MORAL
LITERATURE

(Even today, Jewish little girls are educated in gender roles – fondness
for being looked at, fearlessness in defense of "their people,"
nonsolidarity with their sex – through masquerading as Queen Esther
at Purim; I have a snapshot of myself at about five, barefoot in
the pretty "Queen Esther" dress my grandmother made [white satin,
gold spangles], making a careful eyes-down toe-pointed curtsey at
[presumably] my father, who is manifest in the picture only as the
flashgun that hurls my shadow, pillaring up tall and black, over the
dwarfed sofa onto the wall behind me.)

(Sedgwick 1990: 82)

In this autobiographical fragment from Eve Kosofsky Sedgwick's
The Epistemology of the Closet, set in a discussion of Racine's *Esther*
tragedy, the parentheses do more to highlight than to bracket off her
experience of being framed by Esther at Purim. In this self-reflection
one finds no trace of the capacity for subversion that I have described
in the masquerade of Purim, no dislocation in the system that
projects and fixates on her primarily as benchmark for man's own
identity. Here, the experience of dislocation is one that objectifies
and disembodies: from "solidarity with their sex" for the sake of
"their people," setting the girl off as the privileged object of the
father's veiled gaze.

In certain hands, or with certain lenses, biblical literature can
become an effective lever for establishing normative gender roles, and
Esther is no exception. But the effectiveness of this literature is
always a matter of its *use*, that is, its interpretation, within a larger
constellation of texts and institutions, which work together to
provide the bases or justifications for a particular system of social
relations (e.g., a sexual politics). Biblical literature becomes a powerful tool for social ordering when it is networked into a larger

apparatus, to borrow from Michel Foucault. Such an apparatus both supports certain representations of gender, ethnicity, and so on, and is supported by them (Foucault 1977: 194–7). We find a most striking example today of how biblical literature can be used within such an apparatus in the Christian Coalition movement, which claims the Christian Bible as the sole univocal guarantee for the social order it seeks to establish, but which in fact depends on a much broader network of assumptions and ideological investments that hide behind that big, leather-bound, zippered-up Book.[1]

Although some may view the Christian Coalition as an extreme example, it represents a much more common tendency in contemporary culture – both within and without the academy – to conceive of biblical literature primarily as *moral* literature, that is, as literature that provides role models and guidelines for how to live one's life, socially, sexually, spiritually, and so on. With regard to the book of Esther, this tendency is clearly and poignantly evident in the passage from Sedgwick. And we must not forget that, although it is primarily in non-Jewish interpretive circles that one finds moralistic *repudiations* of the Jewishness of the text, both Jewish and Christian traditions have used Esther to shore up normative representations of women as objectively beautiful, passive, obedient, self-sacrificing, and loyal – in contrast, of course, to Vashti.

The tendency to think of the Bible generally and Esther specifically as moral literature is also evident on the political and religious left, in feminist and gender studies in Esther. For the most part, this scholarship falls into the category of what Toril Moi and others have called "images of women" criticism, which is "the study of female stereotypes in male writing" (Moi 1985: 42), and which has tended to criticize those images as inauthentic when compared with both historical and contemporary women's "real" lives and experiences. As Moi writes (1985: 44–5), "one quickly becomes aware of the fact that to study 'images of women' in fiction is equivalent to studying false images of women. . . . The 'image' of women in literature is invariably defined in opposition to the 'real person' whom literature somehow never quite manages to convey to the reader."

Although somewhat in conflict with this demand for realism, "images of women" criticism also has carried with it a demand for fictional representations of women *role models*. Moi writes (1985: 47), "The feminist reader of this period not only wants to see her own experiences mirrored in fiction, but strives to identify with strong, impressive female characters." Cheri Register (1975: 20) puts it well with regard to the issue of "feminine identity" and the reader's identification with women in fiction: "A literary work should provide *role models*, instill a positive sense of feminine identity by portraying women who are 'self-actualizing, whose identities are not dependent on men.'"

THE WOMAN'S BIBLE AND BEYOND

Whether called "images of women" criticism or something else, this field of research is precisely where feminist criticism of Esther has been, thus far, most productive – from Elizabeth Cady Stanton's *The Woman's Bible* at the end of the nineteenth century (1895; 1898) to *The Women's Bible Commentary* at the end of the present century (Newsom and Ringe 1992). That is, the two dominating interests have been: (1) whether or not the story's plot and characters are realistic and thus believable, when compared to other historical data and to one's own experience; and (2), relatedly, whether the book offers good or bad (liberative or oppressive) role models. Throughout this scholarship, as in studies concerning the Jewishness of the text (see the Introduction), the primary focus is on the book's evaluation as moral literature. In a sense, this focus reveals a continued interest to struggle with issues of biblical authority. At the same time, it has detracted from a more radical study of how gender identities are formed in the first place, and how these formations become deeply problematic, especially when they are exploited in narrative texts, and especially when they converge with other codes of identity such as ethnicity. Thus the retention of gender as a central interpretive category, from pre-feminist writing to the present, has, for the most part, bracketed out critical consideration both of how gender identities are constructed and of the problematic nature of those constructions.

The commentary on Esther by Elizabeth Cady Stanton and Lucinda B. Chandler (one of the members of Stanton's team of contributors) in *The Woman's Bible* (1898: 84–92) is a classic example. While the two writers differ in important ways, both are especially positive toward Vashti and, albeit to a lesser degree, Esther as role models. In Stanton's retelling (which is quite imaginative in its gap-filling[2]), both Vashti and Esther are listed as members of the "grand types," along with Deborah and Huldah, although in her introduction Esther is not included in this list (1895: 13). She mourns the loss of Vashti, "who scorned the Apostle's command, 'Wives, obey your husbands'" (1898: 86). Esther, who was "of rare intelligence" with "wisdom and virtue," "profited by the example of Vashti, and saw the good policy of at least making a show of obedience in all things" (1898: 89; cf. White 1989).

Chandler's comments, arranged alternatively with Stanton's in the same volume, are similar. Vashti's divinely intelligent and dignified character is contrasted against the purely "sensual," anti-intellectual, and gratuitous character of the men at the party, especially Ahasuerus. Refusing to be exhibited as one of the king's possessions, "Vashti is conspicuous as the first woman recorded whose self-respect and courage enabled her to act contrary to the will of her husband. She was the first 'woman who dared'" (1898: 86–7). "Vashti stands out a sublime representative of self-centred womanhood. Rising to the heights of self-consciousness and of self-respect, . . . she is true to the Divine aspirations of her nature" (88). For Chandler, then, Vashti is an unreservedly superior role model for, and great precursor to, the turn-of-the-century women's liberation movement. Esther, too, is highly regarded, as "queenly, noble, and self-sacrificing," although Chandler comments that she was pulled down by her involvement with the power- and passion-hungry king (92).

Beyond Stanton, Chandler also develops a more explicit position with regard to the *realism* of the story, which gives her work further affinity with "images of women" feminist criticism. She argues that the story is most certainly realistic, in relation to both ancient Persia and her own time. She writes, for example, "The truth of the historical record of the men of those days is indisputable. Down to the present the average man sums up his estimate of woman by her 'looks'" (91). The text is also accurate, in her view, with regard to base male sensuality over against female intellect and spirituality. Indeed, this she sees as part of the larger dialectical progress of human history, within which male domination will ultimately be overcome as "womanliness asserts itself and begins to revolt and to throw off the yoke of sensualism and of tyranny" (87). Vashti, she proclaims, is "the prototype" of this "higher unfoldment of woman" (87).

Here, then, as in Anderson's (1950) representations of Jews and Judaism discussed earlier, the dynamic of identity/non-identity comes to play a key part in a particular version of dialectical redemptive history – a historical framework that, in fact, pervades the late nineteenth-century liberalism of *The Woman's Bible*. In Vashti, as Chandler reads her, we can see the Spirit (i.e., "the Divine aspirations of her nature") that will continue to unfold through the March of History into her ideal. The ideal will eventually become the real, as the negativity of male sensualism and brute dominance fade away into the "primitive" or "savage" past. At the end of the nineteenth century, perhaps the peak of modernist Western optimism, Chandler is able to find in Vashti the seeds of what was then perceived to be blooming into the higher life of the mind/spirit, which would liberate women from their physical bondage under barbaric male brute force.

Although the approach of Stanton and Chandler in *The Woman's Bible* remains paradigmatic for the kind of "images of women" criticism that continues to dominate feminist studies in Esther, as in the Bible generally, their positive evaluations have not always been shared. Others are far more critical, especially with regard to the character of Esther (e.g., Esther Fuchs 1982: 149–60; cf. 1985; and Alice Laffey 1988). A more negative view is often taken by non-biblicists as well. For example, Simone de Beauvoir, discussing the ways woman is mythologized in male writing as the archetypal mediator and conciliator, writes,

> [Esther is] pliant to the commands of Mordecai, ... her weakness, her timidity, her modesty she can conquer through loyalty to the Cause, which is hers since it is her master's; in her devotion she acquires a strength that makes of her the most valuable of instruments. On the human plane she thus appears to draw her grandeur from her very subordination.
>
> (1989: 229)

Within feminist biblical criticism, Esther Fuchs is the most stringent proponent of this negative evaluation of the book. The more positive view of Esther as a model, on the other hand, has been championed recently by Sidnie Ann White (1989: 161–77; cf. 1992: 124–9) and Michael V. Fox (1991b: 205–11).[3] A comparison and contrast of these three makes it very clear that feminist criticism of Esther continues to operate along the lines of "images of women" criticism, and in this sense has remained very close to the field marked out by Stanton and Chandler in *The Woman's Bible*. Indeed, the very titles of these three recent studies demonstrate this. White's article is "Esther: A *Feminine Model* for Jewish Diaspora"; the article by Fuchs is titled "*Status* and *Role of Female Heroines* in the Biblical Narrative"; and Fox's "excursus" argument (1991b: 105–211) against

Fuchs is actually titled "*The Image of Woman* in the Book of Esther" (emphasis added).

Fuchs begins, as do the others, with the assumption that Esther is obviously intended to be a model. For Fuchs, however, this model is irredeemably patriarchal. The Esther story, for her, undergirds patriarchal assumptions that women should be deferential, obedient, and beautiful objects for men. Esther can only be a heroine by maintaining these traits and thus remaining within the patriarchal order of things.[4] Fuchs also argues that the lack of any obvious religious strength or awareness of the deity in the character of Esther reflects and supports the "biblical policy" of refusing women access to God and to divine blessing except through childbirth (cf. Fuchs 1989: 151–66). Finally, Fuchs contrasts Esther's timidity and obedience (apparently based on Esther 2) against Mordecai's bold rebellion in the face of Haman (Esther 3 and 5). Vashti, for Fuchs, is another story. Rather than being a model, however, Fuchs argues that the biblical narrative uses her as an object lesson concerning what happens to women when they refuse to participate under the rules of patriarchy.[5]

Fox (1991b) and White (1989) counter the position of Fuchs by reorienting the focus and intent of the modeling. They see Esther specifically as a model for Jews in diaspora. She models how to operate within the system in order to bring about social and political transformation. Fox points out that Fuchs's reading requires one to overlook several details of the biblical text, including the fact that Mordecai, too, is irreligious (as are, in fact, all the characters in the story); moreover, in chapter 4, Esther gives commands to Mordecai and Mordecai obeys. Fox argues, therefore, that Fuchs focuses on early details about Esther's "pliancy and some of her tactics as her essential features and assumes that the author elevates these all to objects of emulation" (1991b: 207).

Both Fox and White, moreover, are justifiably concerned to emphasize context – both the book's context within diaspora Judaism in Persia, and Esther's initial "situatedness" within the story world, which allows her very limited choices. Fox writes (1991b: 207),

> Esther is indeed, at least at the start, a "stereotypical woman in a man's world" (Laffey 1988: 216); but that does not mean that the book teaches (as Laffey would have it) "full compliance with patriarchy." Rather, it teaches that even a stereotypical

woman in a world of laughably stereotypical males is capable of facing the ultimate national crisis and diverting the royal power to her own ends.

Here, as elsewhere, one readily discerns that the issues of "images of women" criticism remain dominant. Indeed, Fox concludes his "excursus" on the image of woman in Esther with a quote from Chandler's comments in *The Woman's Bible* (Fox 1991b: 211).

Certainly, the advantages offered by this kind of feminist criticism in biblical studies should not be overlooked. With regard to what Moi (1985) describes as the demand for authenticity, or "real" images, for example, it enables the critic to emphasize how writers select particular details and omit others in order to present and idealize a fictional universe which supports particular ideological interests. And one must not dismiss the potential uses to which this text can and does lend itself. The book of Esther comes to us marked and remarked as moral literature. Thus it remains a powerful boundary marker for assigning gender roles in contemporary (especially conservative religious) sexual politics. This fact by itself is reason enough for feminist biblical scholarship to continue struggling and asking questions from the perspective of "images of women" criticism.

Yet by centering on biblical literature (in Esther and elsewhere) primarily as moral literature, and by maintaining gender as a key interpretive code (rather than as a problematic constellation of textual constructions), the "images of women" approach of feminist biblical criticism has imposed interpretive limits as well. In the middle of his "excursus" (on his way from Fuchs back to Stanton), Fox (1991b: 209) makes a comment about the book of Esther that begins to point beyond what has been possible within that critical field. With reference to Vashti's insubordination and subsequent banishment in Esther 1, he suggests that the book of Esther is "the only one in the Bible with a conscious and sustained interest in sexual politics," and that its author neither assumes nor supports a patriarchal order, but rather "*perceives the cracks in the façade of male dominance*" (emphasis added).

Fox's comment implies one of the greatest disadvantages of the "images of women" approach, one that is clear in the Esther studies I have discussed here. That is, it tends away from close exegetical study of particular textual details, and instead makes broad sweeps across the surfaces of the text. Interpretation of this sort presents clear, two-dimensional figures, which face one another from opposite sides of the street, and which can be either raised or razed depending on whether they are judged to be good or bad models. Yet close attention to textual details enables one to perceive cracks in those rather superficial façades.[6] As a result, the order of things, and the identities it secures, appear far less self-evident, far less essential, and far more problematic.

Concerning this disadvantage in "images of women" criticism, Moi (1985: 45) writes,

> Such a view resolutely refuses to consider textual production as a highly complex, "over-determined" process with many different and conflicting literary and non-literary determinants (historical, political, social, ideological, institutional, generic, psychological and so on). Instead, writing is seen as a more or less faithful reproduction of an external reality to which we all have equal and unbiased access, and which therefore enables us to criticize the author on the grounds that he or she has created an incorrect model of the reality we somehow all know.

An example from Fuchs's reading of Esther will help to demonstrate this problem. As noted above, Fuchs rightly notices an early juxtaposition in the story between Esther's passive, subordinate obedience to Mordecai and the eunuchs on the one hand, and Mordecai's bold insurrection against Haman on the other. And yet, as will be seen in the next chapter, there are affinities between this other Jew and the insurrectory other woman Vashti: in fact, the pattern of Mordecai's refusal, Haman's rage, and his return to happiness after legislating the exscription of all Jews, closely parallels the pattern of events involving Vashti and Ahasuerus in Esther 1. Thus Mordecai is identified with Vashti, an insubordinate non-Jewish woman. This and other textual details suggest a kind of "feminization" of Mordecai and "Judaization" of Vashti. Given the gynophobic-xenophobic male dread attached to foreign women elsewhere in biblical literature as "that most disturbing of Others" (Fewell and Gunn [1993: 167]), this is an extraordinary identification. When one begins to pick at this loose thread, among others, a great deal of the social-political fabric being presented in the story begins to unravel.

The same will hold true for Esther. To approach her character as a model leads one to read her as a static image, a single-frame type. Yet, as was evident in the narrative of her conscription (in Esther 2), she is from the start multiple, an aggregate of selves that may not be mutually compatible. Neither will she be a static figure, unchanging throughout the narrative, as Fox has pointed out. In fact, her next interchange with Mordecai will involve a role-reversal, in which she does the commanding and Mordecai does the obeying. The closer one looks, the less fixed her image appears.

Unfortunately, then, the "images of women" approach has tended away from close textual work that could begin to expose, even dynamite (to make dynamic, and to explode), the foundations and limits of gender-identity politics, despite what I will argue is a particular hospitality to such an approach in the book of Esther. Moi proposes a more exegetical kind of feminist criticism, described as "a deconstruction of sexual identity" (1985: 14). By this, Moi suggests that feminist criticism must learn to theorize both itself and the patriarchal order in which it is always already located. This requires, Moi writes, "a more sophisticated account of the contradictory, fragmentary nature of patriarchal ideology.... Feminists must be able to account for the paradoxically productive aspects of patri- archal ideology (the moments in which the ideology backfires on itself, as it were) as well as for its obvious oppressive implications" (1985: 64). Drucilla Cornell (1992) has renamed deconstruction the "philosophy of the limit," by which she suggests a mode of criticism that attends to the very limits of philosophical understanding and metaphysical reflection. I have suggested that deconstruction in biblical studies might better be considered as "*exegesis* of the limit."[7] I agree with Moi that without such a practice, criticism easily assumes an essential, self-evident oppositional difference between female/ feminine and male/masculine identity, and, in so doing, winds up relying unawares on the implicit basis of the sexual-political logic of binary opposition. Because scholarship has tended to approach the book of Esther as moral literature, focusing on evaluation of its images of Jew and woman as models, there has been only accidental attention to the problematics of either ethnic or gender identity, let alone to the problematic convergences of the two. Yet the book of Esther is *riddled* with such convergences, ambivalences, and ambigu- ities. As the narrative progresses, they do not disappear or fall out into some neat and tidy resolution, but rather compound and complicate to such an extent that one must ask whether the book of Esther is less about the definition and fixation of identity and more about its problematization.

As we read Esther in this light, not as moral literature but as a strange, sometimes farcical and sometimes deadly serious book of questions, we may find ourselves asking new questions too. For example, is it the self-evidence, the "real" distinctive difference of the one over against the other that, throughout history, has elicited the politics of hatred, genocide, and/or gynocide? Or is it the ambiguities of identity, so difficult for so many of us to accept, the instability of the self and the image of the not-self it projects? How does desire come into play – the desire for an other, for a clear sense of self, for a clearly definable problem? And as the desire for a definable problem leads to the desire for a final solution, how does desire turn to objectification, and then to alienation, and then to a cold violence? And what about the question of identity and social agency? Must one have a clear, integrated sense of one's own identity in order to act in transformative ways? These questions are as critical today as they were for Jews in the early diaspora.

4

WRITING OUT, II

Haman said to King Ahasuerus, "One people diverge, scattered and divided among the peoples in all the provinces of your kingdom. And their laws are different from every other people, and they never do the laws of the king. And, as concerns the king, there must be no willingness to tolerate them. If it pleases the king, let it be written for their annihilation" . . . and it was written according to all that Haman commanded, to the satraps of the king and to the governors who were over each and every province, and to the chiefs of every people of every province, according to its script, and every people according to its language. It was written in the name of King Ahasuerus, and sealed with the king's signet. And the writings were sent out by the runners to all provinces of the king, to wipe out, to slaughter, and to annihilate all Jews, from youngest to oldest, children and women, in a single day.

(Est 3:8–9, 12–13)

Throughout European history, the formation and stabilization of national identity has often depended on projections of the Jew as a nation's image of otherness. "Our nation," whether Haman's Persia or Martin Luther's Germany or Pat Buchanan's America, has often meant "not-Jew," our nation's sense of original and future greatness understood over against a projected image of the odd, always out-of-place, wandering, exiled Jew. But look into the mechanisms of projection, and one invariably finds a heap of texts that inscribe no pristine national origins, but rather a history of painful and violent erasings: of affinities with and indeterminacies in the other who is projected, but also of instabilities and ambivalences in the self who projects that other.

As a window onto such mechanisms of projection, Esther is remarkable, even uncanny. For one, although many argue that such projections of the other Jew find their roots ultimately in the

Christian Church's simultaneous debt to and renunciation of Judaism, Esther was composed centuries before Christianity (almost certainly by the fourth century BCE). Moreover, it is a *Jewish* text that tells the story of an anti-Jew's strategic attempt to annihilate all Jews as the nation's quintessential not-self. That is, it is a Jewish self-representation as other, and as such it cannot help but represent the inherent ambiguities in the Jewish identity being projected.

Finally, as will be seen in this chapter, Esther opens an opportunity to reflect on convergences between others – namely the other woman and the other Jew – and therefore to explore interrelations between representations of gender and ethnicity that are constructed in the name of national identity. Certainly the Jew has not been the only one to bear this dubious privilege of being the other within. Likewise in Esther. In this chapter I want to show how the other woman and the other Jew in Esther are made to occupy the same political space in the architecture of nationalism – that of anomaly, abjection and, ultimately, if all goes as intended, oblivion. Memucan's vision of the other woman and Haman's vision of the other Jew are projected onto each other, onto the same screen, producing a kind of Judaization of the other woman and feminization of the other Jew. As this becomes visible, so do the ambiguities and instabilities in the images of Jewish identity and gender identity that are being created in the process.

THRESHOLD IDENTITIES

This episode begins on thresholds, on the edges that mark the inside off from the outside, on the in-between. This is where Mordecai appears. After Esther was gathered with the other young women in the harem, recall that Mordecai was found "walking to and fro in front of the enclosure" (2:11; on which see above). In 2:19, he was described "sitting at the king's gate." At 2:21, Mordecai is found there yet again. In fact, it appears that Mordecai's *place* in the world of the narrative is always on the edge or periphery, on borderlines. Mordecai is neither inside nor outside, but is always found along the edges, gazing in, keeping his eyes fixed on Esther, whose circulation inside the palace walls is of some interest to himself. Esther is the link between Mordecai and the king. But what of Mordecai's desires? What might he want? The reader is given no clear indication. Sitting at the gate, on the margins of the city and of the page, looking in, Mordecai's interest remains visible but unreadable.

Interestingly enough, those whom he meets while sitting at the gate are two eunuchs, Bigthan and Teresh, "keepers of the threshold" (*mishomrei hassap*; 2:21).[1] These eunuchs are keepers of a threshold in two senses. First, in terms of the physical space being mapped out in this story world, they "keep" or "guard" the gate; that is, they stand at the threshold of the way into the center of royal power. Second, in terms of the sexual identities being constructed within this story world, they occupy the threshold between male and female identities. They are ambiguous within the binary logic of sexual difference, by their lack of the privileged sign of the male sex, but also by the lack of a location as head of household within the family economy – a key dimension, as already noted, in Memucan's sexual politics (1:16–20).[2] (And remember that Mordecai, too, like the eunuchs, is oddly without a wife and family of his own, which is highly unusual for men in biblical narrative). The eunuchs straddle the boundary of sexual opposition. They occupy the blurry region of the in-between. In fact, the eunuchs have appeared in similar situations of betweenness in previous episodes as well, functioning invariably as the intermediaries between the sexes: Vashti was to be brought in and shared between the king and the other men by the seven eunuchs, and the king reiterates that she refused to come "by the hand of the eunuchs" (1:15); similarly, in 2:1–18, the eunuchs "keep" the women at halfway houses which lead into and back out of the king's house.

As sexually ambiguous figures, the eunuchs function in Esther as go-betweens for the two sexes. They occupy the interstice, the limin along the inside edge of the male/female logic of opposition. They hold the threshold line between the sexes, the line that marks oppositional sexual difference; they also, most literally, regularly and repeatedly transgress (cross over) that line. What will become clear at this point in the narrative is that there is a tremendous capacity for political transgression, too, in this (non-)place that is not necessarily accessible by those with clear subject positions within the world of the narrative. That is, they represent not only sexual ambiguity but also, to a degree *because* of their sexual ambiguity, a locus of upheaval and subversion. In the day-to-day business of the palace, however, the king makes much use of them, and thus opens another avenue for subversion.[3] This potential will be nearly realized at the end of chapter 2, as we shall see, and it will continue to play its way through the entire narrative.

Bigthan and Teresh "became wrathful," just as Ahasuerus had at Vashti's refusal (1:12), and sought to assassinate the king (2:21). Being there on the threshold with them, the plan was known to Mordecai as well, and he "revealed" it to Esther the queen (2:22). Whether he had known it for a while and only decided to disclose it once he had a connection with the king (i.e., once Esther was queen) cannot be determined, although the narrative sequence continues to encourage such suspicions. At any rate, Esther informs the king "on behalf of [lit. 'in the name of'] Mordecai" (2:22b), and that is the end of Bigthan and Teresh: "The thing was sought out and both were hanged on a stake, and it was written in the book of the matters of the days [or annals] in the presence of the king" (2:23). That particular coup fails. Still this episode introduces a new dimension of threat to the Persian polis from yet another quarter. Moreover, one must not forget that Mordecai was there "on the threshold" as well, and was identified closely enough with them to have been aware of the plot. Ironically, moreover, because of his connections both to their subversion and to Esther inside the palace, Mordecai's name (although nothing more) finds its way through the palace doors and into the official records.

Expected here might be some recognition by the king of Mordecai's good deed as informant. No such luck. Oddly, the king immediately "made great" and "lifted up" *Haman*, who until now was unknown in the story, "and placed his seat over all the chiefs who were with him" (3:1). Given what has immediately preceded, and given the king's general pattern of immediate reaction, this appears inappropriate. The sense of inappropriateness is further sharpened by the word used to describe the promotion, *nasa'* ("lifted up"), which is related to the word used to describe the king's "gifts" in response to Esther's "gaining" or "raising" (also *nasa'*) favor and loyalty (2:18). It appears almost as if Haman is getting Mordecai's reward.

Within the narrative this royal action sets up a competitive tension between Mordecai and Haman.[4] This tension and its tragic dimensions are compounded by the fact that Haman is identified as an Agagite. As noted earlier, moreover, Mordecai was introduced as a Benjamite (2:5). Within the intertextual field of the Bible, Haman and Mordecai are thus identified with Agag (king of the Amalekites) and Saul, and the tension between them is identified with the conflict in 1 Samuel 15, after which Saul's kingdom began its fated and rapid decline.[5] This not only further compounds the potential conflict between Mordecai and Haman but also threatens a similarly fated end for Mordecai – as well as for Haman, since Agag was ultimately cut to pieces.

WRITING OUT: HERS AND HIS

What follows in 3:2–15 is a narrative sequence that is strikingly parallel to the story of Vashti's refusal and exscription in 1:10–22. Everyone is honoring Haman. Mordecai, however, disclosed as a Jew, refuses to do so. Haman, who hates Jews, is enraged; he recommends that all Jews be exterminated by law, as oppositional to the king's law; the king agrees, "if it pleases" Haman; the recommended plan of action is set in motion and Haman and Ahasuerus sit down to drink. Thus here, as in chapter 1, the movement is from public exhibition of greatness, to refusal by an other, to rage, to a recommendation that will restore the former order of things, to the return of pleasure and drinking. What this enables in the book of Esther is an astonishing identification of the newly introduced Jewish insurrectory hero, Mordecai, as the other Jew over against the law of Haman and the king, with the previous heroine, the non-Jewish insurrectory woman Vashti, as the other woman over against the law of Memucan and the king.

The parallel pattern begins in Est 3:2a: "All the other servants who were at the gate of the king were bowing down and doing obeisance before Haman, for thus the king had commanded."[6] Not surprisingly, Mordecai is there, as usual, with the others "at the gate of the king." He, however, "did not bow down and did not do obeisance" (3:2b). As in the interchange between the king and Vashti, Mordecai's refusal here is not direct, but is mediated through a collective of others. Unlike the story of Vashti's refusal, however, here the actual interchanges between this group and the transgressor are described:

> And the servants of the king who were at the gate of the king said to Mordecai, "Why are you transgressing [cf. 1:19] the command of the king?" And although they talked to him day after day, he did not heed them. So they revealed [it] to Haman, to see whether the words of Mordecai would stand, for he had revealed to them that he was Jewish.

> (3:3–4)

Back in Esther 1, Memucan made explicit precisely what the problem was with Vashti's refusal. It had to do with the transgression of her place as woman within the king's household, which in turn grounded the same household economy throughout the kingdom. Here, it appears that the intensity of the scandal of Mordecai's refusal has to do with his being Jewish – something that he, unlike Esther, has "revealed" (*nagad*). But ambiguities arise here as well. First, why did he need to reveal that he was Jewish? This notice, along with the fact that Esther has thus far intentionally "not revealed her people," suggests again that Jewish identity is not immediately self-evident. Second, why did he reveal his Jewish identity at all? Why not avoid revelation, as he commanded Esther to do? Here again, as with Mordecai's desires, he remains highly visible yet unreadable, even in the act of self-revealing.

Moreover, just as Mordecai had "revealed" (*nagad*) news of the two eunuchs' planned insurrection (2:22), so now the other opportunistic servants at the gate "reveal" (again, *nagad*) Mordecai's insurrection to Haman. In this way, *Haman and the king* are identified with one another over against Mordecai the insurrectory Jew and Vashti the insurrectory woman.[7]

Mordecai's refusal fills Haman with "rage" (*hemah*), the same rage that burned in Ahasuerus when he heard about Vashti's refusal. Clearly, the issue in Haman's case is not one that concerns sexual politics, but it does have something to do with Mordecai's Jewishness, thus invoking yet another dimension of identity politics in the story. This dimension is confirmed in verse 6:

> But he regarded with contempt [lit. "despised with his eyes," contrasting "pleasing to look at"][8] the thought of laying a hand himself on Mordecai, for they had revealed to him Mordecai's people, and Haman sought to wipe out all the Jews throughout the kingdom of Ahasuerus, that is, Mordecai's people.

At least part of the reason for Haman's rage at Mordecai's refusal, then, is due to Mordecai's identification with the Jews ("that is, Mordecai's people"), whom Haman loathes and seeks to obliterate. Thus, just as the scandal of Vashti's refusal was necessarily linked to her place, her identity, within the social order, so it is with Mordecai.

In 1:16–20, the solution to the subject's rage was offered by an advisor (Memucan). Here in 3:7–10, however, the pattern is altered slightly: Haman himself makes a proposal to the king for legal action that will calm his own rage. This, of course, suggests an identification of Haman with Memucan (an identification that the Targums of Esther advance even further).[9] As with Memucan's proposal, it appears that Mordecai's particular transgression will be used by Haman as a springboard for a far more expansive, even universal, program of annihilation based on an identity politics structured oppositionally over against the other Jew. Thus, whereas Vashti's transgression and the action taken against her served to exscribe her, while simultaneously reinscribing the king's and Memucan's sexual politics, here Mordecai's particular transgression serves Haman's larger political interest in wiping out all Jews as quintessential not-selves, oppositional to "our" law and order. Indeed, his words to the king in 3:8 make this explicit:

> One people diverge, scattered and divided among the peoples in all the provinces of your kingdom. And their laws are different from every other people, and they never do the laws of the king. And, as concerns the king, there must be no willingness to tolerate them.

In a few words, those who are admittedly scattered and divided, difficult to locate, are fixed as the one people (*'am 'ehad*) that is divergent, anomalous (outside the king's law and order), projected as the nation's dubiously privileged image of alterity. The manyness implied by "scattered and divided" is reduced to a single divergence. The Jew is fixed in Haman's discourse as *the* heterogeneous element in an otherwise homogeneous nation.

Ahasuerus, who has yet to turn down a proposal (and in fact never will), approves Haman the Jew-hater's request that it "be written for their [the Jews'] annihilation" (3:9),[10] and offers him full support, "as is pleasing in your eyes" (3:10–11). Thus Haman's rage is replaced with pleasure, as the scribes are called in to "write according to all that Haman commanded" (3:12). And, just as with the previous writing, which exscribed Vashti while reinscribing patriarchal domination, so this new exscription of the Jews is "sent out" (3:13; cf. 1:22) to "every province, according to its script, and every people according to its language" (3:12; cf. 1:22), exscribing all Jews and attempting to reinscribe national identity and homogeneity (i.e., as "ethnic cleansing").

Of course, within the story world and even historically speaking, all other Persians besides the Jews were not of one *ethnos*. The ancient Persian empire was in fact very diverse, as Haman himself indicates (by adding "to every people according to its language" etc.). Rather, with regard to Haman's (and the king's, insofar as he accepts it) identity politics, all divergence and opposition to "us" and "our law" is *projected* here onto the other Jew. Therefore to remove Jews, in this fantasy, is to remove opposition; what remains is unity, sameness.

Whereas the first law in chapter 1 was brutally explicit concerning its sexual politics ("every man should act as chief in his house"), so here the orders are chilling: "to wipe out, to slaughter, and to annihilate all Jews, from youngest to oldest, children and women, in a single day [*yôm 'ehad*; one day for one people] . . . and to plunder them for spoil" (3:13). Additionally, copies of the writing were then issued "as law in each and every province for all people to be prepared for that day" (3:14).

This episode concludes (3:15), as one might expect, with a return to drinking. As the couriers drive furiously about with the new "royal word" (as in 1:19), and as the law is given in the acropolis of Susa, "the king and Haman sat to drink." Here again, as in the incident with Vashti, once the proposal is approved and carried out in all the provinces, abatement of rage and return to rest is marked by drinking. Here, the drinking also confirms *Haman's identification with the king*, over against the Jews who are about to be annihilated. Yet there are signs of chaos breaking in, which, as before, suggest that things aren't so secure as they appear from within the palace walls: "the king and Haman sat to drink, *but the city of Susa was in turmoil*."[11]

Haman's identification with the king at the center of royal power is thus created over against the projection of the other Jew. The self who projects his other becomes visible even as the other does. Images of self and not-self emerge simultaneously, and grow sharper in non-relation to each other. It is a double emergence. But the double emergence of the self and his abject is also a double erasing, for images of the one and the other become more sharply defined as the ambiguities in each of them and the overlaps between them are erased. The ambivalences and indeterminacies in the other Jew, which make him difficult to locate and define (indicated by Haman in his phrase "scattered and divided" [3:8]), must be erased in order to reduce him to the nation's quintessential perversion of law and order. At the same time, the self's own ambivalences, his own spillings-over into the other, and the ambiguities in his own sense of identity with the king and royal power, must be erased.

On this strategic double erasure, enacted in Haman's speech, Jonathan Magonet has been particularly insightful. Drawing on the intertextual relations between Mordecai/Haman in Esther and

Saul/Amalek in 1 Samuel 15, discussed earlier, he focuses not on the Jew in the text but rather on the character of *Haman*:

> We forget that the information that he is an Agagite tells us not only that he comes from the line of Israel's enemies, but also that *he, too, is an outsider* in the Persian court. When he speaks of the people scattered throughout the land whose laws are different from those of every other people (3:8), he is also *describing, in a projection, some aspect of his own outsider status*. For Haman, too, is insecure, part of a minority group, relying on his wealth or other keys to power to maintain his position, ready to invent a scapegoat to insure the continuance of his power. Haman is nothing more than the *alternative face of Mordecai, a distorted reflection* of the same character ... and perhaps it is that deeper relationship that Rava is pointing towards when he says that a man is obliged to drink so much wine on Purim that he becomes incapable of knowing whether he is cursing Haman or blessing Mordecai.
>
> (1980: 175; emphasis added)

It is not Mordecai's distinctiveness as a Jew in-and-of-itself, over against Haman, that brings on hatred. Rather, it is Haman's *identity with* Mordecai as mutual outsiders, *other* to the present political regime, that in turn leads to Haman's projection of what he hates about himself onto Mordecai and the Jews. Mordecai is Haman's negative image. In this sense, Esther is not about the distinctiveness of the Jew over against Haman, but the *ambiguity* of identity, the fuzzy area between and among identities.

As overlappings between Haman and Mordecai have become apparent, moreover, so have overlaps between the Jew and another other, Vashti. In both cases, the objective of the subject (Haman and the king here; the king and his men, especially Memucan, in Esther 1) is to define his own greatness and consolidate national identity over against them, and in both cases the other is reduced to a commodity of exchange between men, used to advance other identity political interests. In both cases, the end result of exscription is (1) the identification of the advisor with the king, and (2) the establishment and shoring up of a larger identity-political ordering of power (one based on sexual identity and one based on ethnic identity).

Yet another issue with regard to the politics of ethnic identity in Esther emerges again at this point, namely, the paradox of diaspora identity: to be *dispersed* and *one* simultaneously. I have mentioned Esther's successful and seemingly effortless concealment of her people (she simply does not disclose it), as well as Mordecai's apparent need to *reveal* his Jewish identity in order for it to be known by the servants and by Haman. By attending to these actions of revealing and not revealing, the text introduces a most basic problematic into any identity-political program based on Jewish identity, as is Haman's. Despite his clear delineation of us and them, there is in Haman's speech on the "Jewish problem" (3:8; quoted above) also an inadvertent admission of the problematics embedded in his own logic: this one, isolatable, ethnic divergence ("One people diverge") in the order of things is admittedly also "scattered and divided" among all the people everywhere.

5

FINDING ONESELF
SIGNED UP

The aim of any "final solution," which is always first to isolate what does not fit into the privileged image of the self and then to eradicate any trace of it, will always be impossible to achieve. Because the solution's problem, construed as the "Jewish problem" or otherwise, is fictional from the start. Because the problem of the other is the problem of the self. Because the anomalous, the strange, the foreign, the savage – whether projected onto the unfamiliar wilderness of the book of Esther, or onto the dark continent of the other woman, or onto the perverse strangeness of the other Jew – is always *within* as well as *beyond* the self who struggles to eradicate it. Self intertwines with stranger and stranger intertwines with self. The intertwining is irreducible, within Esther, within Haman, within Luther, within me, within you, within us. Total integration into a homogeneous whole is impossible. So is total segregation. Otherness can never be absorbed or eradicated entirely.

This irreducible, finally insoluble intertwining and multiplicity of self and other is what we see when we look into the mechanisms of projection. Here is a meeting-place between reading the book of Esther and reading Luce Irigaray, whose *Speculum of the Other Woman* (1985a) opens our eyes to an otherness beyond reduction or erasure, beyond objectification or abjection.

WITHOUT HAVING BEGUN TO PLAY

All these are interpretive modalities of the female function rigorously postulated by the pursuit of a certain game for which she will always find herself signed up without having begun to play. Set between – at least – two, or two half, men. A hinge bending according to their exchanges. A reserve supply of *negativity* sustaining the articulation of their moves, or refusals to move, in a partly fictional progress toward the mastery of power.

(Irigaray 1985a: 22)

When Esther arrives, the playing-field is already marked off. The rules are set. And let Vashti be the example of what happens when those rules are transgressed. Esther is signed up in a sort of game without having begun to play. Her function is to be the pleasing object of the male gaze and the quintessential object of exchange between the king and his men, to replace Vashti, who had refused to be exchanged between the king and his men and thereby had not reflected well. Esther is signed up to play the part Vashti had refused to play. And so she ostensibly does, at least in the beginning.

As discussed earlier, feminist studies have tended to approach Esther's conscription from an "images of women" perspective, focusing on her character as a good or bad role model. This chapter begins to develop a space for conversation between biblical studies and gender studies where different questions – about the unstable constructions of gender and ethnicity – can be articulated. These questions are of two general kinds: (1) how individual identities are shaped and fixed within particular symbolic and social orders; and (2) how individual agents *exceed* their fixed positions within a particular order, indicating instabilities in that order and making social transformation possible. Like Beauvoir before her, Irigaray attends to the mechanisms of gender formation that project woman as man's quintessential object, over against which he defines himself. But Irigaray moves significantly beyond Beauvoir in emphasizing the male subject's *vulnerable dependence* on the other woman as negative image, or benchmark, for his own self-construal. Irigaray highlights a fundamental insecurity in the subject who projects the other woman as fixed object – an insecurity that is evident in projections of *both* the other woman and the other Jew in Esther.

BACKGROUNDING THE SUBJECT

Irigaray's *Speculum of the Other Woman* (1985a) is a book of converses, speaking to, with, and against towering figures like Freud and Plato "about women." But *Speculum*, along with her other books, is also in conversation with contemporary figures not always addressed by name. One is Simone de Beauvoir, whom Irigaray herself regarded as a major precursor. (In *Je, Tu, Nous* [1993: 10], she describes

61

her disappointment when, after sending Beauvoir a copy of *Speculum* "in which I wrote an inscription to her as if to an older sister, she never replied.") Another partner, never mentioned by name in *Speculum*, is Jacques Lacan (she was expelled from his École Freudienne de Paris and from her faculty post at Vincennes upon publication of *Speculum* – reminiscent of the king's reaction to Vashti).[1] Yet another partner, rarely recognized in discussions of Irigaray's work, but important to her conception of otherness, is the philosopher and Talmudist Emmanuel Levinas. In Irigaray's relation to each of these figures, among others, there are both strong affinities and radical differences, and it will be important to discuss her engagements with them in order to understand the significance of her work for larger academic discussions on philosophy, linguistics, and psychoanalysis, and in order to put her work into conversation with Esther.

Like Irigaray, Emmanuel Levinas emphasizes the irreducibility of otherness, and understands one's confrontation with the particular face of the other as an ethical moment. For Levinas, much of the history of Western philosophy has been characterized by a drive to dominate and comprehend all difference through identification and unity, or sameness. That is, it "reduces the other to the same," thereby neutralizing alterity (1969: 42). This logic of the same is totalitarian. It aims at grasping all things – containing, controlling, totalizing, making self-present and intelligible. Anything that is non-identical must be absorbed by force into the identical (1969: 42–8); otherwise, it must be either exterminated or abjected (cast out of the system of representation as neither subject nor object). But otherness persists in its irreducible particularity. Indeed, the irreducible difference of the other is the precondition of identity, which means that a subject's responsibility to the other must be primary, demanding that one, relentlessly and vigilantly, thinks the limits of any totalizing system. Thus "the overflowing of an adequate idea" (Levinas 1969: 80) becomes an ethical moment: a moment of obligation to and responsibility for an other. In this way Levinas draws our attention to the particular that exceeds systematization and is beyond accommodation by general categories.

In an often overlooked footnote to her first use of the term "Other" in *The Second Sex* (1989: xxviii), Beauvoir comments on the implicit androcentrism in an early speculation by Levinas (from *Time and the Other* [1947; English trans. 1987]) on the feminine as "Other," man's mystery, "of the same rank as consciousness but of opposite meaning." Although she clearly rejects this and other statements by Levinas that define woman in relation to masculine privilege, Irigaray has continued Beauvoir's critical engagement of Levinas in two more recent essays (1986; 1991). Irigaray shows how, in his association of the unknown, unknowable other with femininity, Levinas's ethical subject becomes necessarily male. At the same time, the feminine other in Levinas's writing remains to some extent an unembodied ideal for the ethical subject, an other in relation to which he will always fail (here, on this reading of Levinas, is some affinity with Lacan). Therefore the relation of the feminine other becomes purposive for the male subject's own becoming. "In this transformation of the flesh of the other into his own temporality, it is clear that the masculine subject loses the feminine as other" (1991: 110; cf. 1986).[2] By man's necessary failure in this ethical relation, moreover, the "other sex ... would represent the possible locus of the definition of the fault, of imperfection, of the unheard, of the unfulfilled, etc." (1991: 112). Irigaray insists on the particularity of the embodied "other of sexual difference" (1991: 112), against an idealized "feminine," and focuses on the ethical moment as the embracing love-relation between the two sexes – not a confusion of the one and the other, but an unpredictable, open-ended relation in which the other sex as irreducible other remains fundamentally unknown and unexpected (1986: 231, 238).[3]

Although Levinas slides into an androcentric oppositional form of reductionism of the feminine to man's other at points in *Time and the Other*, in his discussion of the caress in *Totality and Infinity* (1969), and elsewhere[4] (and while this is, as Cornell [1992: 87] puts it, "Hegelian to the core"), there are other elements of Levinas's work that are fiercely anti-Hegelian and that would counter his move here. As I have already mentioned, a primary force of Levinas's work has been to safeguard the unknowability of the other, and to reject violent reductionisms of the face of the other to an object of exchange within the economy of the same. Thus Irigaray's reading is best understood as a *citation of Levinas against Levinas*. Levinas's own writings, in their self-critical resistance to totalizing discourse, invite such a reading.

Levinas's critique of the logic of sameness in philosophy, which aims to neutralize alterity, is strikingly similar to Irigaray's critical analysis of the logic of sameness in philosophical and psychoanalytical discourse on the other woman. Her *Speculum* opens with a reading, or hearing, of Freud's lecture on "Femininity," which articulates his view that boys and girls develop sexually in the same way (1985a: 11–129; cf. 1985b: 34–5). In this model of sexual development, the girl is ultimately doomed to become man's quintessential negative image, or lack, "an inferior little man" (1985a: 25), over against which he conceives of himself.[5] Analyzing this psychoanalytic scheme, Irigaray discovers a process of specula(riza)tion that involves a progressive splitting-out from a single (male subjective) origin into a series of binary oppositions – light/dark, in/out, and especially male/non-male, phallus/lack, positive/negative, active/passive – in short, a *symbolic structure* of Western sexual identity politics. (These are the "interpretive modalities" that she refers to in the passage quoted earlier.) Within this dynamic of identity-building, as Beauvoir had also made clear, woman is fixed as the quintessential object for the subject to bounce off; for the subject needs an objectivity, in order to discover, fulfill, and save himself, a solid ground from which he can spring into transcendence. "If there is no more 'earth' to press down/repress, to work, to represent, but also and always to desire (for one's own), . . . then what pedestal remains for the ex-sistence of the 'subject'?" (1985a: 133)

The significance of Freud in Irigaray's argument is not that he *introduced* this "law of the self-same" into theoretical discourse (she shows its operations in Plato, too, for example), but that he has articulated it most explicitly in the context of modern intellectual discourse. As she puts it in a subsequent interview concerning her *Speculum* (1985b: 69),

Why this critique of Freud?
Because in the process of elaborating a theory of sexuality, Freud brought to light something that had been operative all along though it remained implicit, hidden, unknown: *the sexual indifference that underlies the truth of any science, the logic of every discourse.* This is readily apparent in the way Freud defines female sexuality. In fact, this sexuality is never defined with respect to any sex but the masculine . . . in the imaginary and symbolic workings of a society and a culture. The "feminine" is always described in terms of deficiency or atrophy, as the other side of the sex that alone holds monopoly on value: the male sex.

Although Freud is the named object of critique, Irigaray's *Speculum* is also an interrogation of the work of Jacques Lacan, a powerfully influential scholar-analyst, and a contemporary of Irigaray in the

64

early 1970s. In conversation with structural linguistics and anthropology (especially Ferdinand de Saussure and Claude Lévi-Strauss), Lacan develops a theoretical discourse that foregrounds the psychosexual development of the human subject, that subject's place in the social order, and, most significantly, how all of this relates to language (i.e., symbolic order), as the system in which the subject takes intelligible shape. Put another way, Lacan develops a model for understanding how the *diachronic* movement of psychosexual development brings the human subject to the point of taking up a position within the *synchronic* social and symbolic order described by early structuralists. Thus he was able to "delineate the symbolic articulation" (Irigaray 1985b: 61) of the psychoanalytic model of human development.

For Lacan, the psychosexual development of the human subject involves a series of stages, moving one from a pre-linguistic, undifferentiated, androgeneous whole – imagined by Lacan via Aristophanes's myth of the circle people in Plato's *Symposium* (e.g., Lacan 1981: 205) – to a particular position (e.g., as male, heterosexual, etc.) within the social-symbolic order. Each phase of this process, from one's birth to one's entry into language to one's negotiation of the Oedipal complex,[6] entails an experience of loss (of full identification with one's self, one's world, one's mother, etc.), and the sense of fragmentation and lack that results from this process is what engenders desire.[7]

Lacan construes the social-symbolic order and the subjective positions within it in structuralist terms, that is, in terms of a closed, binary system of oppositional differences, with the unconscious itself structured according to the same binary oppositional code. On this point, the beginning of section 2 of Lacan's "The Freudian Unconscious and Ours" (in 1981: 20–1) is worth quoting from at length:

> Most of you will have some idea of what I mean when I say – *the unconscious is structured like a language*. This statement refers to a field that is much more accessible to us today than at the time of Freud. . . . Before any experience, before any individual deduction, even before those collective experiences that may be related only to social needs are inscribed in it, something organizes this field, inscribes initial lines of force. . . . Before strictly human relations are established, certain relations have already been determined. They are taken from whatever nature may offer as supports, supports that are

arranged in themes of opposition. Nature provides – I must use the word – signifiers, and these signifiers organize human relations in a creative way, providing them with structures and shaping them. . . . [I]t is this linguistic structure that gives its status to the unconscious. It is this structure, in any case, that assures us that there is, beneath the term unconscious, something definable, accessible and objectifiable.[8]

For Lacan, this structural foundation not only provides stability and grounding for the present social-symbolic order, but also legitimates and guarantees psychoanalysis as a science (much as structuralist linguistics does for many literary analysts).

Implicitly in *Speculum*, and more explicitly elsewhere, Irigaray argues that the system delineated by Lacan is inherently phallocratic. Whether or not one agrees with this critique depends on one's reading of Lacan's use of the term "Phallus," by which he refers to the privileged signifier in the social-symbolic order, signifying a completeness which everyone desires and which everyone lacks.[9] If its significance is meant to be sexually neutral, as orthodox Lacanians insist, why use this term, loaded as it is? (Certainly a Lacanian could never say that it is *"just* a metaphor.") To what extent does the significance of "Phallus" slide inevitably into the significance of "penis," and thus from Phallus to penis to maleness? Is Lacan not, so to speak, asking for it? Whether or not it is a misreading to call Lacan a phallocrat, I would suggest that his use of this term, along with his linking of psychoanalysis to structuralism, *at least* risks shoring up Freud's androcentric logic of the same as integral to Lacan's understanding of the social-symbolic order. At any rate, the critical force of *Irigaray's* interrogation of Lacan's Phallus is evident in the following passage, for example, which concludes her essay, "Psychoanalytic Theory: Another Look" (in 1985b: 34–67):

What role has been marked off for her in the *organization of property, the philosophical systems, the religious mythologies* that have dominated the West for centuries?

In this perspective, we might suspect the *phallus* (Phallus) of being the *contemporary figure of a god jealous of his pre-rogatives*; we might suspect it of claiming, on this basis, to be the ultimate meaning of all discourse, the standard of truth and propriety, in particular as regards sex, the signifier and/or the ultimate signified of all desire, in addition to continuing, as emblem and agent of the patriarchal system, to shore up the name of the father (Father).

By showing how sexual development and identity are related to structures of language and society, Lacan shows that sexual identity is social-symbolic, and not simply a matter of biology. Irigaray's engagement with Lacan recognizes this (e.g., 1985b: 61) but moves beyond his investments in structuralism, evident in much of his work, drawing greater attention to (1) the problematic limits, and deconstruction, of the symbolic order being delineated, and (2) the narrowly androcentric, unilinear, and homogeneous description of psychosexual development common in the models of both Freud and Lacan.

Against the reduction of woman to the "other side" of man – to Man's Other within the Logic/Law of the Same – Irigaray asserts the non-oppositional difference, the absolute, utterly embodied alterity, of the other woman, that is, an alterity that refuses to be reduced to an object of exchange within the male sexual economy (e.g., 1985b: 30–1).

In this sense, I would argue, there are divergences from Lacan and Beauvoir that place Irigaray's writing into closer relation with the best of Levinas as described above.[10] In Beauvoir, woman as "Other" and woman as "object" are basically identical (i.e., the second sex). For Irigaray, however, otherness is not entirely reducible to the (male) subject's object; and thus there is within it the potential to break apart the very binary opposition that it has been made to guarantee: "But what if the 'object' started to speak? Which also means to 'see,' etc. What disaggregation of the subject would that entail?" (1985a: 135) What if the ground moves and shakes? What if the mirror becomes concave, like a speculum?[11] This upsets the entire phallocratic economy, which requires a solid grounding of fixed objects and oppositions. Reduction of otherness in service of self-construal is rendered impossible. The oppositional structure begins to collapse, and new possibilities of relation within the political begin to emerge.

For Irigaray, the irreducible otherness of the other woman carries with it a power to resist reduction. This is so because alterity can never be reduced fully to oppositional difference (as the subject's object), and therefore the problematics of patriarchal identity politics are always open to deconstruction.[12] There is a kind of unknowable, unmasterable, unpredictable alterity in the relation between the one and the other which replaces sexual opposition and which cannot be contained under categories of identity.

Although Irigaray focuses on the ethical relation to the other within sexual politics, her work is highly suggestive of the specularization of the "other Jew" by Haman in the book of Esther as well. As Magonet (1980) suggested, Haman projects all otherness onto the Jews as his and the nation's ultimate vision of alterity; over against them he positions himself in full identification with the Persian king and his law and order. In so doing, the other Jew is *reduced* to an object of exchange in the relation between the two men, Haman and Ahasuerus, like the "hinge" that is "set between two, or two half, men" in the quotation from Irigaray above.

It should be remembered that Levinas himself was Jewish, writing during and after the Nazi Shoah, and that his biography is "dominated by the presentiment and memory of the Nazi horror" (1978: 177). His parents were killed in Lithuania, and he himself only narrowly escaped the same end, having moved to France as a teenager. (Ironically, as a World War II prisoner-of-war survivor, his French military uniform made his own identity ambiguous enough to save him from the Nazi death camps.) As Susan A. Handelman (1991: 178) points out, Levinas's *Otherwise than Being* (1981) is dedicated to those 6,000,000 Jews killed by the Nazis, and to the "millions of all confessions and all nations, victims of the same hatred of the other man, the same anti-semitism." When reading Levinas, one cannot help but think of the face of the other Jew sentenced to obliteration under the sign of a Nazi "final solution."

Both Irigaray and Levinas attend to an otherness that escapes the projections and fixations of Haman as well as Memucan, emphasizing how otherness can be neither subsumed into sameness nor reduced to oppositional difference. Indeed, their work suggests a deep insecurity in the self that would project such visions of alterity, showing how the solidity of one's own identity depends precariously on the fixity of the other-as-object.

> Subjectivity denied to woman: indisputably this provides the financial backing for every irreducible constitution as an object. . . . Once imagine that woman imagines and the object loses its fixed, obsessional character. As a bench mark that is ultimately more crucial than the subject, for he can sustain himself only by bouncing back off some objectiveness, some objective.
>
> (Irigaray 1985a: 133)

Within this dynamic, the subject's identity, whether that of Memucan/king/nation over against the other woman, or Haman/king/nation over against the other Jew, depends on an impossible fixation.

ANOTHER PLACE

The next episode in the book of Esther is the encounter between Mordecai and Esther following the decree to annihilate all Jews (Esther 4). How does this episode look when it is read through Irigaray's *Speculum*? First, it becomes clear that Esther, a woman whom we begin to imagine imagining, is no longer so securely fixed as man's benchmark, no longer denied subjectivity. Second, we see Mordecai's own fixation on Esther beginning to slip even as he is objectified and marked for annihilation as the other Jew by Haman and the king.

As previously discussed, at her initial conscription in chapter 2, Esther is, by all surface appearances, utterly deferential. She is the ideal woman-as-pleasing-object of male exchange, contrasted explicitly against Vashti's subversion (i.e., she is "instead of Vashti"; 2:4, 17). This dimension of her sexual identity has been most evident in her relation to Mordecai. She conceals her identity as Jew and as adopted daughter of Mordecai, for example, "because Mordecai commanded her [*tsivvah 'aleyha*] not to reveal" (2:10, 20). Indeed, the text indicates that she obeys Mordecai while in the harem "just as when she was raised by him" (2:20). Mordecai does the taking and the commanding; Esther is taken and obeys.

This relation to Mordecai changes, however, in chapter 4, by which time she (still without "revealing her people") has come into a new identity as queen within the Persian court, and by which time Mordecai (after "revealing his people") and all other Jews have come to be marked for oblivion by law. At this point Mordecai's (and, by association, all Jews') dependence on and potential political identification with Esther becomes clear. Without her, he and the other Jews may be doomed to a fate worse than Vashti's. This has been presaged by Mordecai's continued interest in Esther, gazing in from the margins as she was taken away from him into the king's domain. As I commented earlier, Esther's circulation within the palace is Mordecai's most promising investment. And yet, as Irigaray suggests, such investments in her as object of exchange indicate the insecurity of his own position as well.

"Once imagine that woman imagines and the object loses its fixed, obsessional character" (Irigaray 1985a: 133). In this episode Mordecai begins to imagine that Esther is in fact imagining, hatching plans of her own which are not readily available to him. Indeed, as I have noted, the text suggests that she has been imagining all along, through strategies of appearance, without disrupting the superficial order of ostensible power and authority. As we will soon see, her unexplained directives to Mordecai in this episode will effectively distance her from Mordecai's fixed, obsessional watch on her. At the same time, Mordecai's dependence on her as an absolutely crucial benchmark for his own sustenance and that of all other Jews will become more pronounced.

Mordecai, upon hearing the new law instigated by Haman, tears his clothing, puts on sackcloth and ashes, and goes "through the city crying out loudly and bitterly" (4:1), as do all Jews "in every province" (4:3). When this is revealed (as before, *nagad*) to her, "the queen" (not "Esther" but "the queen") does *not* join in solidarity with the other Jews in sackcloth and wailing, but instead becomes "greatly agitated."[13] Instead of joining Mordecai in this behavior (a social performance which would effectively identify her with him), or even tolerating it, she sends new clothes to Mordecai, imploring him to change his look and his ways. She does not know that he has revealed himself as a Jew to the eunuchs and Haman, and therefore, as far as she knows, sackcloth is the only thing that is exposing him as such (not because only Jews wear sackcloth, of course, but because he is openly mourning the decree calling for the annihilation of all Jews). If he puts on the clothes she sends, his Jewish identity, like hers, will once again be hidden.

Mordecai's affrontive behavior here verges on a most open and direct form of transgression: he comes into the city and right up to the threshold (the king's gate) in sackcloth and ashes, despite the law that "no one should enter the king's gate dressed in sackcloth" (4:2). He is threatening to transgress a royal boundary. But what is it more precisely that bothers Esther so much about his behavior? Is Esther agitated because his action puts him in a risky situation (either by identifying himself as Jew or by transgressing the law against entering the gate in such fashion)? Or is she agitated by the fact that he is threatening to cross one of *her* boundaries? Thus far he has had no access to her royal sphere of existence, and has not approached its boundary to cross it. He has only looked in from the outside. Is he now getting too close to the line?

Mordecai refuses to don the clothes sent by Esther. This refusal, like those of the past, begins yet another interchange, this time between Esther inside the palace and Mordecai on the threshold (once again in the vicinity of the gate; 4:6). Here again, moreover, as in past interchanges between the sexes, a eunuch, Hathach, is summoned by Esther to be mediator. The two are separated by space (one inside the gate, the other outside), status (one a Persian queen undisclosed as Jew, the other disclosed as Jew and marked as such for death by Persian law), and sexual difference. The eunuch, ambiguous with regard to sexual identity, status (a servant who is at the same time privy to high-level information), and physical location (crossing back and forth through the palace gate), is their mediator, the one who bridges their separation. As the quintessential boundary-crosser and threshold-keeper, he both ensures and jeopardizes communication.

Mordecai tells all to Hathach (4:7), shows a copy of the written law, and sends Hathach "to command her" (again, *le tsavvot 'aleyha*) to go to the king (4:8). One expects that, as usual, what follows will be a report of her unequivocal deference to Mordecai's command. This time, however, Esther talks back (4:11), via Hathach, instructing Mordecai in the law, perhaps trying to reassert it against both Mordecai's potential transgression and the transgression he is demanding of her.

> All the king's servants and the people of the king's provinces know that if any person, man or woman, comes into the king's presence in the inner court without having been called, there is one law for that person: death. Only if the king extends his golden scepter may that person live. I myself have not been called to come to the king these thirty days.

In one sense, this is a long way of saying no. Everyone knows that one does not go into the presence of (*lipnê*) the king when one has not been called there. Thanks to Vashti, moreover, it is equally clear that one does not *not* come when one *is* called. In one sense, Esther's words here remember Vashti's transgression of such laws and protocol. In another sense, however, these words, "revealed" (4:12) to Mordecai indirectly by the eunuch, put further distance between herself and Mordecai, and make his investment in her less secure. The fact that this is threatening to Mordecai is evidenced by the threat implied in his return message:

Do not imagine that you will escape with your life, in the house
of the king, from all the Jews. For if you indeed keep silence at
this time, relief and deliverance will come for the Jews from
another place, and *you* and your father's house will perish. But
who knows whether for a time like this you have attained to
royalty?

(4:13–14)

Mordecai makes clear that, as far as he is concerned, the alternative
to helping the Jews is death. By using the language of "escape"
(*malat*) and "deliverance" (*natsal*), moreover, the rhetoric casts
Esther's doom in terms of a judgment day for the Jews. In this light,
the phrase "from all the Jews" has a double meaning. On the one
hand, it might be understood to be asserting Esther's *identity with*
the Jews who are to be annihilated (this is the common understanding
of it); that is, "don't imagine you'll get away any more than the rest
of us simply because you're in good with the king now." On the
other hand, its implication may be more sinister, namely, that Esther
will not escape from "judgment" *at the hands of the Jews themselves.*
That is, she and her father's house will not escape certain annihilation
when Jewish deliverance comes from "another place." Indeed, this
is the simplest translation, given the actual word order in the text:
"Do not imagine / with your life / you will escape / in the house of
the king / from all the Jews." By mentioning the demise of her
father's house, moreover, Mordecai is making the threat quite
personal. Recall that when Esther's parents died, Mordecai took her
to himself "as his own daughter" (2:7). She is all there is left of her
father's house. Who, if not Mordecai as foster parent, has kept
Esther's father's house from perishing thus far? Mordecai thus
asserts his claim on her, and then threatens to deny her and her
father's house, once the deliverance begins, if she does not help now.

Most commentators read deliverance "from another place"
(*mimmaqôm 'aher*) as a veiled reference to God (e.g., Moore 1971:
50, 52; Paton 1908a: 222; Ringgren 1958: 131). Although this possibility should not be ruled out, I suggest that the potential revolu-
tionary connotations of such deliverance (whether involving divine
intervention or not) should not be overlooked by such a postulation
either. We have seen how *location* has played an important part in
the formation of identities and power relations throughout the story.
Might it be that Mordecai, who is always located on the margins and
often identified with marginal characters – such as the "keepers of

the threshold" who threatened revolution earlier – knows of another place from whence real blood-and-guts deliverance might come?

Whatever the case may be, Mordecai gives Esther no explicit instructions, and neither does she ask for them. Rather, she appears to be imagining a strategy of her own, which, in fact, she never "reveals" to Mordecai. From here on, Mordecai will remain on the margins and in the dark, and Esther will keep him there. She tells Mordecai,

> Go [lek], gather [kᵉnôs] all the Jews who are found in Susa, and fast [tsûmû] on my behalf. Do not eat or drink for three days, night or day. I and my servants will likewise fast. In this manner I will go to the king, which is not legal. And if I die, I die.
>
> (4:16)

Clearly Esther has heard Mordecai's threat and has taken it seriously. She will transgress the law she has just stipulated (4:12; thus identifying herself with Vashti?), and if she dies ('abad; the same verb used in Mordecai's threat on her father's house), so be it. Nonetheless, Esther's reply (4:16) remains forceful, beginning with a string of three imperatives directed to Mordecai and the other Jews ("go," "gather," and "fast").

In immediate response to Esther's imperatives, and without a word back, "Mordecai crossed [back] over and did everything just as Esther had commanded" (4:17). Significantly, this statement draws several elements from the language that was used in chapter 2 to describe *Esther's* obedience to *Mordecai*. In 2:10 it is written that Esther did not "reveal" her Jewish identity "because Mordecai commanded her [tsivvah 'aleyha] not to reveal it." And in 2:20, "Esther did ['osah] what Mordecai said." Now, Mordecai "does" (ya'as, the same verb in another form) everything that Esther "commands him" (tsivtah 'alayw). From here on, Mordecai hangs in the balance, as Esther becomes the key player. Mordecai knows she has a plan, and so do readers, but it will remain indecipherable until it is carried out.

Esther finds herself signed up in someone else's game, an object of ogle and exchange between men, written into the story as the antithesis of the other woman Vashti. She is conscripted to be the king's new benchmark; she is also Mordecai's benchmark. At this point, however, she begins to swerve from her script, and in the process her actions and plans are increasingly illegible. As she swerves, moreover, as she begins to imagine in ways that are unreadable, the insecurities of those men who depend on her (the king, the nation, Mordecai, her people) are increasingly plain.

6

INSOMNIA AND A LOST
DREAM OF WRITING

Mordecai and Esther have parted ways once again. The next time
Mordecai will present himself to Esther, all the important work will
have been done: Haman (not Mordecai) will be hanging on the stake
meant for Mordecai, and Esther (not Mordecai) will be in charge of
his estate (8:1). But before then: two face-to-face encounters with
royal law (one involving Esther and the king [5:1–8], the other
involving Mordecai and Haman [5:9–14]) and a royal bout with
insomnia, in which sleep is not all that is lost.

FACES TO FACES

On the third day Esther put on her royal robes and stood in the
inner court of the king's palace, facing the inside of the king's
palace. The king was sitting on his royal throne in the royal
palace, facing the opening of the palace. And when the king saw
Queen Esther standing in the court, she gained favor in his eyes.
The king extended to Esther the golden scepter that was in his
hand. Esther approached and touched the tip of the scepter.
And the king said to her, "What for you, Queen Esther? What
do you seek? Up to half the kingdom I will give to you."

(5: 1–3)

"The face to face remains an ultimate situation" (Levinas 1969: 81).
Levinas turns us toward the face-to-face encounter as a profoundly
ethical moment: the particularity of the face of the other invokes a
sense of responsibility, even obligation. As such, it is a moment that
is both freighted – an ethical encounter with the particular face of the
other that can lead to new life or ultimate demise – and, simultaneously, mundane. So it is with the following encounter between

75

Esther and the king, which is both the beginning of Esther's subversion of the law to annihilate all Jews and the lampooning of a self-absorbed, impulsive king who would do anything for a beautiful woman with her hand – or her lips – on his scepter.[1]

One may also find in this encounter traces, or erasure marks, of that other woman Vashti, who refused to be the object of this same ogling king. Like Vashti, Esther will transgress the law (5:1–2; cf. 4:11). Hers is a quite physical transgression: as she transgresses (crosses over) the threshold of the inner court so she transgresses the law (5:1–2), which prescribes death to any woman or man who enters the inner court unbidden by the king (4:11). Like Vashti's transgression, too (and *unlike* Mordecai's in the previous episode), Esther's transgression will risk no one's life but her own. Unlike Vashti, however, Esther transgresses by *coming before* (*lipnê*, "to the face of") the king, sans eunuchs, rather than by refusing to come (cf. 1:12). She insists on being a subject in the same way that Vashti had refused to be an object.

Esther puts on her royal garb and crosses over the threshold and into the inner court, literally "facing" the king in the entrance of the palace (5:1).[2] Immediately she "gains his favor," as she has on earlier occasions. Then, in a highly suggestive and richly innuendoed gesture, the pleased king "extended to Esther the golden scepter that was in his hand. Esther approached and touched the tip of the scepter" (5:2). The king asks what she seeks, offering her even as much as half his kingdom (5:3).[3]

This face-to-face (and hand-to-scepter) encounter resembles the crucial evening encounter between Ruth and Boaz on the threshing floor (Ruth 3). Ruth, too, transgressed by coming to the threshing floor that evening (as is apparent from Boaz's concern the next morning; see Ruth 3:14). Then, when Boaz is full of food and drink, Ruth "came softly and uncovered his feet" – a common biblical euphemism for male genitalia (Ruth 3:7–8). Boaz awakes, startled ("behold, a woman at his feet!"), and asks what she wants. So begins a conversation that marks the turning point in Ruth's otherwise potentially ill-fated life. Now compare this encounter with that of Esther and the king in Esther 5: (1) in both cases the woman initiates the encounter by transgression of both a physical boundary and a prohibition (into the inner court and onto the threshing floor); (2) in both cases her action sets up an encounter involving sexual innuendo and male vulnerability (hand on the king's extended scepter and a woman lying at Boaz's exposed "feet"); (3) in both cases the man, who is at the center of ostensible power, asks the woman to voice her interest; and (4) in both cases the woman does so, and this leads to a series of events that ultimately brings about a reversal of fortune.

Esther is operating in spaces neither organized nor consolidated along the lines of the king's more ostensible royal power structure. Here again questions arise concerning the nature of power, and especially concerning the relation of power to authority. Authority, represented by the king, is a consolidation of ostensible political power. But power in Esther cannot be reduced to authority. Royal authority cannot consolidate every point of power and identify it with the king. Indeed, as was clear especially in Esther 1, even the ostensible power that the king does have is often represented in farcical fashion.

There remain, therefore, points of resistance which retain transformative and even subversive potential. Mordecai operates, albeit negatively, in the domain of ostensible power, which is identified with authority: he refuses to honor those whom the king honors, he brings secret plans for assassination to light, and he challenges royal law in the most public way. In fact, the battle between Haman and Mordecai operates entirely on the level of public edicts (to honor Haman, to kill all Jews, to prohibit certain public displays of mourning, and eventually to honor Mordecai [6:1–11; 8:1–2]). Vashti's refusal, likewise, was a most public resistance to ostensible royal power. In this domain, both Vashti and Mordecai have been largely unsuccessful. Esther, on the other hand, has shown no resistance in this public domain. Her power is not yet manifest in that realm, but is gathering force in areas that remain hidden beyond its field of vision.

The king's offer to fulfill her bidding leads not to revelation but deferral; her only request at this point is to "let your majesty and Haman come to the drinking party I am throwing for him" (5:4). Like both Vashti and the king before her, then, Esther will "throw" (or "make/prepare"; 'asah) a mishteh (cf. 1:3, 5, 9; 2:18). The request appears modest, to say the least, considering that she is standing before the king with her hand on his extended scepter after being offered half his kingdom. Indeed, as shall soon become clear, it is seductively so, for as the king's and Haman's pleased eyes continue to follow this pleasing object, they (especially Haman) will soon find themselves straying far from where they had expected to be.

At the party, the king again calls on her to make her request, and again offers half his kingdom (5:6). With all due respect, and ever ensuring that it "be pleasing" and "favorable" to the king (5:7), Esther asks that yet another drinking party be planned, again including only the king, herself, and Haman. Then she says she will make her actual request (5:8).

Meanwhile, the narrative turns from Esther's face-to-face, hand-to-scepter encounter with the king to a second face-to-face encounter between Mordecai and Haman (Est 5:9–14). And here again, as in Esther's encounter with the king, Vashti's presence as absence is haunting. But whereas Esther's encounter leads to a party, Mordecai's second encounter with Haman, which comes next in the narrative, leads to the building of a stake on which he is to be executed.

"That day," after Esther's party, "Haman went out happy and pleased of heart" (5:9). Significantly, the phrase "pleased of heart" (*tob leb*) was used previously, in Esther 1, to describe the drunkenly pleased king at the climax of his second party, at which time he had called for Vashti. Haman, too, has just come from a drinking party when he meets Mordecai again. And Haman's good pleasure, like the king's, is again about to be frustrated by Mordecai. Here, then, as in 3:1–15, a pattern emerges involving Haman and Mordecai that places the other Jew Mordecai in a position that identifies him with the other woman Vashti.

Upon encountering Mordecai[4] (again, as usual, "at the gate of the king"), Mordecai "did not rise and did not tremble" (5:9).[5] As with the king after Vashti's refusal in 1:12, and as with Haman previously in 3:5 after Mordecai's first refusal, so here too Mordecai's dishonoring behavior throws Haman into burning rage (again, *hemah*). Haman returns to his own home and sends for his friends and his wife, Zeresh, to come (5:10).[6] In a way similar to the king at the beginning of the first drinking party, he lists off the details contributing to his greatness, including his promotion by the king, and climaxing with his exclusive invitation to the drinking parties with the king and Esther (5:10–12). (Little does he know.) And yet, he complains, the good pleasure of all this is ruined "every time I look at Mordecai *the Jew* sitting at the gate of the king" (5:13). Faced with the other Jew, Haman's own subjective status is threatened.

At this point, Zeresh and the friends (like Memucan in chapter 1; like the servants in chapter 2; like Haman himself in chapter 3) offer a proposal. This time, however, it is not for another writing: "Let a stake be made fifty cubits high, and in the morning tell the king, and have Mordecai hanged on it. Then go with the king to the drinking party happy" (5:14). As with the king in 1:21 and 2:4, so here "the word was pleasing" to Háman, and he did just as they recommended, looking forward to drinking with the king yet again (cf. 3:15). The language here is nearly identical to that describing the king's reaction to and implementation of Memucan's plan with regard to Vashti.

Thus, as in chapter 3, the pattern of relation between Haman and the other Jew Mordecai parallels the pattern in chapter 1 involving the king and the other woman Vashti. And thus the Jewish hero Mordecai and the non-Jewish heroine Vashti are once again identified with one another. At the same time, the text also insinuates a possible identification of Mordecai with the two insurrectory eunuchs, Bigthan and Teresh, keepers of the threshold, whose coup failed and who were hanged by the king. Mordecai has been identified with them already to some extent, insofar as he was privy to their secret assassination plans (2:21–3). On the other hand, his revelation of those plans distanced him from them, though that has yet to be fully registered by the king; that is, it has been written in the annals but not read in a way that might publicly recognize Mordecai's actions. Mordecai is once again left in-between: between the king and the corpses of the king's executed enemies, between a writing (in the annals) that identifies him as a friend to the state and another that marks him for annihilation as its most threatening element.

DESERT

Insomnia – the wakefulness in awakening – is disturbed in the core of its formal or categorical *sameness* by the *other*, which tears away at whatever forms a nucleus, a substance of the same, identity, a rest, a presence, a sleep. . . . The other is in the same, and does not alienate the same but awakens it.
(Levinas 1989a: 170; cf. 1989b: 30–6)

Insomnia is being unable to *just be*. It disturbs the stability of being, tearing away at whatever aggregation of features allows me to imagine that I am whole, one, integrated. It is the embodiment of unrest, the settling-in of non-stasis. It is the refusal of rest.

Refusal by whom? By my own body, which is somehow, in the experience of insomnia, other than that same body's desire for sleep. Insomnia, then, is the body divided against itself: the refusal of rest by otherness within the subject, a rustling of what Levinas calls the *il y a*, the "there is" – and what Jewish mysticism calls *yesh* – which calls into question my own identity, my own self-sameness. The irony of the body's refusal of that very same body's desire for sleep elicits a profound sense of self-disaggregation. And this ironic refusal (here life itself is inherently, deeply ironic) becomes an opening to ethics: the stirring of otherness within the one, which is also the stirring of desire, opens the restless subject to other others.

In the next episode of Esther (6:1–13), it is the king's own restlessness, in the form of insomnia, that opens him to the possibility of a new relation to the other, even though he has already sentenced that other to oblivion by law, eliciting a conflict within. With Esther, of course, the other (in the form of the other Jew marked for oblivion by royal law) has been within the palace walls for some time now, identified ironically with the king and Haman. Here a restless night brings otherness into the center yet again.

"On that night sleep deserted the king" (6:1). What night? The night of Esther's drinking party. Did her deferral of her request, a second time, leave him sleepless? What disturbs his rest? Is it her face? When was the last time they had met? In the inner court, when she had risked a face-to-face encounter against the law. When were they together before that? Interestingly enough, the last encounter mentioned in the narrative before the scene in the inner court was when Esther reported the assassination plot "in the name of Mordecai" (2:22). Is this the trace memory that has introduced the other into the king's being? Has Esther's return also recalled Mordecai to the king?

"Sleep deserted." The absence of sleep as wakefulness. Wakefulness as the experience of a desertion, loss, absence. Sleep as presence. As sleep departs, retreats, it leaves behind a desert of wakefulness more disturbing than any nightmare. "There is no trace but in the desert," writes Levinas with Jabès, "The beginning of action is passage, wandering. . . . Leaving familiar, known sites – landscapes, faces – for an unknown place – the desert, the new face" (Jabès with Levinas 1993: 160). Wandering in this wakeful desert, the king comes to rest upon a text: his royal annals, which order his days, his months, his years, marking the passage of time with names and events. He finds the place in the text that marks Mordecai's difference from the eunuch coup: "It was found written what Mordecai had revealed about Bigthan and Teresh, the two eunuchs, keepers of the threshold, who had sought to lay a hand on King Ahasuerus" (6:2). In this reading of this other royal text, Mordecai is dissociated from former marginal insurrections and identified with the center of power.

What follows is rich with irony. The king discovers that Mordecai has not been honored for his deed. (The night thus moves from lack to lack, as lack of sleep reveals lack of due honor.) He asks who is in the court (6:3–4), in order to make amends, to fill the void of obligation left by the other Jew. Immediately following the king's question, the text sharpens the irony by punctuating the coincidence of Haman's entry with quite contrary intentions: "Now Haman had just come into the outer court of the king's palace in order to speak to the king about hanging Mordecai on the stake he had prepared for him" (6:4). At precisely the same moment the king is asking for someone to honor Mordecai, Haman is on his way to ask the king to have him hanged.

The king asks Haman what honor ought to be done for one whom the king desires to honor (6:6). This is the same language that had been used to describe the king's honoring of Haman at the beginning of chapter 3. In both cases, the repetition of the word "honor" (y^eqar) is intriguing, insofar as it suggests that honor is a powerful means of shoring up identity with the king (see also chapter 1, discussed earlier). Back in chapter 3, moreover, the reader's expectation had been denied: just when it would have been appropriate for the king to have honored *Mordecai* for exposing the assassination plot, the king had honored *Haman* instead. Here the irony moves in the opposite direction: Haman, unaware of the previous revelation, assuming full identification with the king, and thus fully expecting that the king wishes to honor *him*, recommends excess:

> For the man whom the king desires to honor, bring royal robes which the king has worn, and the horse which the king has ridden, and on whose head a royal crown is placed. And let the robes and the horse be given over to one of the king's most noble princes. Let him array the man whom the king desires to honor, and let him lead the man on horse through the open square of the city, proclaiming before him, "Thus is it done to the man whom the king desires to honor!"
>
> (6:7–9)

Haman, again seeking the strongest possible identification with the king and royal power, recommends that the honored one be allowed to openly masquerade as king: to wear the royal robes worn by the king, to ride the royal horse ridden by the king. Dress-up time. (That the king would agree to this recommendation, which he does [6:10], is yet another farce on his authority.) Yet Haman's grandiose proposal blows up in his face. The king wishes to honor *Mordecai*, not Haman. Thus Mordecai comes to be identified with the king in the most extraordinary way. Of all people, Mordecai, the other Jew whose refusal to give honor to a Persian high official led to a royal decree for the annihilation of all Jews, now masquerades as king, while Haman parades after him, proclaiming, "Thus is it done to the man whom the king desires to honor!" (6:11)

Mordecai returns to the gate and Haman hurries home in mourning, with his head covered (6:12) – a posture that is strikingly similar to Mordecai's in chapter 4 after the law was written (under the authority of Haman *and* the king) to annihilate all Jews. As Mordecai's public image is transformed from sackcloth and ashes to royal robes, so Haman begins to be transformed in the opposite direction. Back home the words of Zeresh and Haman's "wise ones" (like those advising the king about Vashti in chapter 1) seem to seal this new fateful reversal of fortunes:

> If Mordecai, before whom [*lᵉpanayw*, before whose face] you have begun to fall, is of Jewish seed, then you will not overcome him, but will surely fall before him [*lᵉpanayw*].
>
> (6:13)

This double use of *lipnê* ("to the face of" or "in the presence of") brings the issue of presence and the face-to-face encounter to the fore again, as has been the case in so many other power relations in Esther. Here it focuses the power relation between Haman and Mordecai in terms of Haman's face to face with the other Jew. For Levinas, the face-to-face encounter is understood as a moment of potential transformation for one's ethical relation to the other; here, however, the face of the other brings only horror. Indeed, this passage demonstrates profound insight into a particular dimension of the anti-Jewish subconscious, one bearing uncanny resemblance to more recent manifestations in European and American culture. From the literature and art of the Spanish Inquisition, to Céline's anti-Semitic pamphlets from the 1930s and 1940s, to the revisionist tract stuck under my windshield wiper during a public presentation by Elie Wiesel two winters ago, the anti-Jew's hatred is often fueled by a collective nightmare-fantasy that Jews have some special power, whether in the form of a worldwide conspiracy or something more supernatural. In the process of marking Jews for annihilation, the one doing the marking tends to demonize them, attributing to them some other power to which the anti-Jew has no access. In the context of the book of Esther, however, this too is subjected to irony. The text cannot possibly present this view in an unambiguously serious manner, as a clear affirmation of the special power of "Jewish seed." Indeed, there is the first irony: Mordecai has no seed (or at least has not planted any). Mordecai himself, moreover, has certainly not thus far appeared to be rising in power and prestige. On the contrary, he has been busy digging himself deeper and deeper into trouble, and this new turn for the better, along with Haman's humiliating turn for the worse, has happened largely by accident. Moreover, Jewish identity itself – particularly Mordecai's identity as Jew – has remained fundamentally ambiguous and largely invisible up to this point in the story. It is something that must be revealed to be known. It would be wrong, then, to take this superstitious view about special Jewish power as a straightforward affirmation, any more than one would affirm Haman's construal of the "Jewish problem" in Esther 3, precisely because it relies on assumptions about Jewish identity that are being called into question at every turn.

By the conclusion of the episode, Mordecai is no longer simply the other Jew, marked for death by the law. He is now, *also*, identified with king and royal power (over against marginal insurrection by the "keepers of the threshold," the eunuchs) as an honored doer of memorable deeds. Whereas Vashti's refusal to come and be ogled had frustrated the king, and had led to her dissociation by exscription, here the king's insomnia has opened him to another text (the annals) which inscribes another association with Mordecai. Otherness is thus identified with sameness at the center of ostensible power, revealing a royal body – the king's own self, but also the royal body of writings – divided against itself. On the one hand, as sleep deserted him, in the desert of wakefulness, he found himself wandering through the annals to find the place marking his identification with "Mordecai *the Jew*" (that is what he calls him when speaking to Haman in 6:10). On the other hand, there is another text, written under his authority, that marks the Jew for annihilation and identifies him with oblivion.

Insomnia ends a certain dream of writing as fixed, univocal, irrevocable. As both Danna Nolan Fewell (1992: 11–20) and Mieke Bal (1992: 77–99) have shown, there is a strange preoccupation in Esther with the (im)permanence of writing. Thus far, to *write in* (inscribe) has served primarily to *write out* (exscribe). Written law has been used to exscribe Vashti and others who might think to act like her (Esther 1); and since chapter 3 writing has anticipated the exscription of all Jews as particularly other to royal law and its subjects (Haman and the king). There has been only one minor exception to this form of writing as exscription: the royal record of the exposure of the eunuch assassination plot against the king "in the name of Mordecai" (2:22–3). This writing, of course, runs counter to the joint composition by Haman and the king in chapter 3, which calls for the demise of all Jews. One writes Mordecai as a doer of memorable deeds (6:1) and the other sentences him to oblivion. What determines which writing will be realized? They are mutually incompatible. The record of Mordecai's memorable deed could undo the law against the other Jew – though it has not yet done so. On the other hand, if the law against the other Jew is fulfilled, it will erase Mordecai, leaving his name in the annals without a referent – a signifier whose signified has been buried.

What ultimately determines which writing will undo and which writing will be undone? In the book of Esther it appears to have something to do with accident and coincidence on the one hand, and with the inability to locate and fix otherness on the other hand. On the one hand, chapter 6 of Esther piles on irony after irony by its series of narrative "it-just-so-happened-thats." On the other hand, otherness itself, in the form of the other Jew, appears to keep slipping out of place (as negative image, quintessential not-us) and finding its way inside the palace to be identified, quite problematically, with the king. Insofar as these accidents and slippages undermine political determinations (especially Haman's at this point) that are based on identity and carried out by royal decree, this suggests yet again a profound sense of the problematics of identity politics.

Neither is writing itself so stable as it had once appeared, despite royal pretenses to the contrary. Writing cannot, it now appears, fix identities and determine fates without fail. More is needed to complement writing. It must be actualized by readers, who establish its sense and who enforce its stabilization. The record of Mordecai's deed had been written but not read, or at least had not been read by the right person at the right time. As unread writing – a dead letter – it made no difference. Now that is has been read, however, it may in fact lead to the undoing, or unreading, of Haman's and the king's most deadly letter – a death sentence for the Jews.

7

SUBVERSIVE EXCESSES

The prisons precede me. When I have escaped them, I discover them: when they have cracked and split open beneath my feet.... This is a thought, that we Jewomen have all the time, the thought of good and bad luck, of chance, immigration, and exile.

(Cixous 1993a: 203, 204)

There is no self that is prior to the convergence or who maintains "integrity" prior to its entrance into this conflicted cultural field. There is only the taking up of the tools where they lie, where the very "taking up" is enabled by the tool lying there.

(Butler 1990: 145)

Culture is never a single integrated whole – a locktight prison – within which each member can be reduced to a particular social location; rather, there is only a "conflicted cultural field." None of us within it is reducible to one. Our "location" is interstitial, between identities that are often mutually incompatible. Each of us is a locus of convergences, exceeding any particular cultural conscription and eliciting a sense of identity crisis that can work in socially and politically transformative ways. "Never being simply one," as Irigaray puts it (1985b: 31), can be incendiary. "It's not a question of drawing the contours," writes Hélène Cixous, "*but what escapes the contour*, the secret movement, the breaking, the torment, the unexpected" (1993b: 96). Through readings of Cixous, Foucault, and Butler, this chapter seeks after what escapes. It begins by turning from the story of Esther to that of another exiled "Jewoman," Cixous, and it will lead, in the next chapter, to a new reading of Esther's own coming-out.

WHAT ESCAPES

Cixous's well-known 1975 essay, "The Laugh of the Medusa," is similar to Irigaray's *Speculum*, published a year earlier, in arguing that "sexual opposition, which has always worked for man's profit ... is only a historico-cultural limit" (English trans. 1976: 883). In the same essay, she too is critical of the "place" provisioned to woman within the (implicitly Lacanian articulation of) symbolic order:

> Their "symbolic" exists, it holds power – we, the sowers of disorder, know it only too well. But we are in no way obliged to deposit our lives in their banks of lack, to consider the constitution of the subject in terms of a drama manglingly restaged, to reinstate again and again the religion of the father.
>
> (1976: 884)

Cixous, however, does not "sustain" such an analysis. Indeed, her writing never stays put. In another essay, first published in 1977, she imagines her "capitalist-realist Superuncle," the "Master of Repetition," who sounds something like a market-wise publisher, reprimanding her for this unfixity:

> He repeats his hundredth rescene for me: every year, it's the resame. "We think you're here. And you're there. One day we tell ourselves: this time we've got her, it's her for sure. This woman is in the bag. And we haven't finished pulling the purse strings when we see you come in through another door. Now really, who are you? If you're never the same, how do you expect people to recognize you? Besides, what's your principal name? The public wants to know what it's buying. The unknown just doesn't sell. Our customers demand simplicity. You're always full of doubles, we can't count on you, there is otherness in your sameness. Give us a homogeneous Cixous. You are requested to repeat yourself. Nothing unexpected. A minimum of change for us. Halt! At ease. Repetition!"
>
> (1991: 33)

Cixous's writing resists systematization and reduction to a particular "position." The reason for this, I suggest, is that her work is precisely the kind of poetically transgressive practice called for by others like Irigaray and Kristeva. That is, she is concerned with writing "that produces irreducible effects" (1976: 883), that "blazes *her* trail in the symbolic" (888), and that will therefore remove the "conceptual orthopedics" of sexual opposition. One reason for this focus on writing, she writes, is that literature has traditionally been a place where sexual oppositions have been powerfully exaggerated (note here her awareness of the relation between the social and the symbolic). Therefore, as "guardian of a language which escapes" (1993a: 210), writing is also a crucial site of social-symbolic transformation. Moreover, much like Kristeva, she focuses on writing as a process of transgressive production (see especially 1993b: 91–103), and on the speaking/writing subject as unstable, unfixable, and heterogeneous.

What is particularly provocative in the context of the present discussion is that, for Cixous, the practice of writing and its relation to subjectivity within the social-symbolic order remains closely related to her own self-conception as exiled "Jewoman" (see especially Suleiman 1991: vii–xxii). She was born in Oran, Algeria in 1937 to a German Jewish mother who had fled Germany in 1933 as Hitler took power. Many of her less fortunate family members were deported and murdered in the death camps. Her father, who grew up in a Sephardic Jewish family in Algeria, had the status of an overseas French citizen. He died when she was still young. Turning the psychoanalytic understanding of the pre-Oedipal child's loss of the mother inside-out, she writes, "He who abandons me is my mother. My father dies: thus father you are my mother. My mother remains. In me forever the fighting mother, the enemy of death. My father falls. In me, forever, the father is afraid, the mother resists" (1991: 19–20). While her father was alive she learned Arabic and Hebrew as well as French and German. She recalls, however, that she first became aware of her (non-)identity as a Jew through the experience of anti-Judaism. That is, her first self-conception as Jewish was formed by the denial by the other children of an identification with them. After the war she moved to an Arab neighborhood in Algiers, where her father had his medical practice, and where she again lived as a foreigner. All this made her aware, from earliest memory, of her non-place, her manyness (1993a: 203–4).

> *What* I was, if that could be described, was a whirlwind of tensions, a series of fires, ten thousand scenes of violence (history had nourished me on this: I had the "luck" to take my first steps in the blazing hotbed between two holocausts, in the midst, in the very bosom of racism, to be three years old in

1940, to be Jewish, one part of me in the concentration camps, one part of me in the "colonies").

(1991: 17)

For Cixous, this triple bind of being exile, Jew, and woman – all of which converge in the title "Jewoman" – becomes the scene of writing, of "traversing names" and of stealing/flying (French *voler*) through the cracks in the barriers erected within an identity politics founded and governed by the gynophobic and xenophobic Law of the Father. Levinas writes of the fixation of the subject's being (or status) within the world as the death of the other. Cixous writes of writing as a struggle against death (1976: 876), of resistance to the fixation of the "I" against the other within the death-grip of the Law. "Writing: a way of leaving no space for death, of pushing back forgetfulness. . . . The other is safe as I write" (1991: 3, 4). This is done, largely, by exploiting the problematic convergences of identity, which undermine all effort to keep the "I" in opposition to and at a distance from the not-I. To write as the Jewoman is to be "guardian of a language which escapes" (1993a: 210).

This leads to another issue raised by Irigaray, Cixous, and Butler, one that is explicit in the quotations at the beginning of this chapter. There is in all this a sense of being always already located: "she will always find herself signed up without having begun to play," writes Irigaray (1985a: 133), within the "interpretive modalities" of patriarchal logic so powerfully described by Beauvoir, as an object of exchange between men. Cixous puts it most succinctly: "The prisons precede me" (1993a: 203). Yet here again, I would argue, Irigaray and Cixous diverge from Beauvoir, for they are far less optimistic than Beauvoir that this system will crumble as socialism succeeds. Hence the desire and necessity to disturb the order *from within*, to feel along the surfaces of the prison-house of language for cracks, to encourage deconstruction – or, as Cixous puts it, to follow the error (1993b: 93). That is, "It's not a question of drawing the contours, but *what escapes the contour*" (Cixous 1993b: 96).

To find oneself *signed up* in this game, then, is to be signed up in more ways than one: she is not only enrolled on the books, her name placed according to the phallocratic rankings of a particular sexual politics, but also signed into a differential network of signs, called the symbolic order – an order that can never be stabilized entirely precisely because of these slippery signs.

THE SUBVERSIVENESS OF ET CETERA

A major underlying issue throughout this book, and throughout poststructuralist theory generally, is how – or how *not* – to understand the social and symbolic ordering of culture as a unified whole. What are cultural wholes? Put specifically with regard to the concerns of the present discussion, what is the relation of the social-symbolic order as a whole to the consolidation of *power*? For if power is identified solely with authority within that order, then the possibility of political transformation is eliminated, and the political cynicism toward feminism, for example, which is so prevalent these days, is completely justified.

Such questions have been central in contemporary anthropology as well. Since the initial work on a mediterranean anthropology of honor and sexual identity in the 1960s, for example, it has become increasingly clear that cultures should not be conceived as monolithic or homogeneous "wholes" within which "different aspects ... fit together like the pieces of a jigsaw puzzle" (Peristiany and Pitt-Rivers 1992: 4). Peristiany and Pitt-Rivers summarize this shift in perspective nicely: "we perceived a possible social function to be accorded to paradoxes and ambiguities: culture was no longer a set of rules of conduct followed blindly which supported the organization of society, but a structure of conflicting premises within which struggle for dominance took place" (1992: 4). Implied in this statement, moreover, is that a more simplistic conception of culture leads inevitably to a reductionistic view of power relations, in which power comes to be inextricably linked with law and authority.

By invoking the analytics of power developed by Michel Foucault, Judith Butler has provided a major innovation concerning the relations of power and identity politics in this regard. In the first volume of his *History of Sexuality* (1978; cf. 1984: 51–75), Foucault criticizes what he calls the "juridico-discursive" understanding of power, or "the principle of power-as-law" (1978: 82). This understanding conceives of power as purely negative, a repressive prohibition which seeks to maintain dominance. Thus it can have no productive, transformative capacity.

Foucault argues that this reductionistic representation of power is rooted in the emergence of European monarchies in the Middle Ages. These monarchies sought to consolidate power under their authority in terms of the law. "In political thought and analysis," Foucault writes, "we still have not cut off the head of the king" (1978: 88–9).

Yet there are kinds of power – "points of resistance," as he calls them – which are "irreducible to the representation of law" (89). It follows, therefore, that while the monarchy succeeded largely in consolidating power under law and authority, this consolidation of power must not be equated with power itself. Simply put, power is antecedent to law.

> The analysis, made in terms of power, must not assume that the sovereignty of the state, the form of the law, or the over-all unity of a domination are given at the outset; rather, these are only the terminal forms power takes.
>
> (1978: 92)

Thus Foucault offers a different theory of power, as

> a multiple and mobile field of force relations, wherein far-reaching, but never completely stable, effects of domination are produced.
>
> (1978: 102)

> a multiplicity of force relations immanent in the sphere in which they operate and which constitute their own organization; as the process which, through ceaseless struggles and confrontations, transforms, strengthens, or reverses them; as the support which these force relations find in one another, thus forming a chain or system, or on the contrary, the disjunctions and contradictions which isolate them from one another; and lastly, as the strategies in which they take effect, whose general design or institutional crystallization is embodied in the state apparatus, in the formulation of the law, in the various social hegemonies.
>
> (1978: 92–3; cf. 1984: 61)[1]

Through "ceaseless struggles and confrontations," force relations take form as they are encoded into a larger system of dominance and control, "embodied in the state apparatus, in the formulation of the law, in the various social hegemonies" (1978: 92–3). Power materializes within a particular system, that is, within an apparatus of power/knowledge in which a particular set of force relations depends on a particular conception of society, and vice versa.

> The apparatus is thus always inscribed in a play of power, but is also always linked to certain coordinates of knowledge which issue from it but, to an equal degree, condition it. This is what

the apparatus consists in: strategies of relations of forces supporting, and supported by, types of knowledge.

(1977: 196)

From this perspective, establishment of a political ordering and consolidation of public power, which in Esther is closely linked with monarchy and the law, is understood as a strategy of containment "for integrating these unbalanced, heterogeneous, unstable, and tense force relations" (1978: 93; see also 1977: 194; and Bhabha 1994: 73–5).

Yet, although such an apparatus *works*, it is never completely stable. It is a "terminal form" of power, and its status as "terminal" is always shaky. The apparatus, or "economy of power" (Foucault 1984: 61), is never successful in its effort to totalize, and for this reason revolution is always a possibility. Foucault's analytics of social power is able to make sense of the points of access to power in a text such as Esther that *exceed* royal consolidation. These points of access belong to "the swarm of points of resistance [traversing] social stratifications and individual unities" (1978: 96). Indeed, such points of access are recognized as necessary, for without them social change would be inconceivable.

Working from Foucault's discussions of power and the apparatus, Judith Butler (1990; 1993) focuses specifically on the *materialization* (and *intelligibility*) of gender, sex, and sexuality – including the sexed body itself – and explores how the regulatory system of power relations that creates and enforces a particular materialization can be subverted from within that system. Both constructivist (most often structuralist) and essentialist approaches to sexual identity have tended toward political determinism: whether sexual identity is understood to be formed within a hegemonic cultural system or according to specific essences, these identities appear solidly fixed and destined to be repeated. Moving beyond the old constructivism/ essentialism debate, Butler sees culture as fundamentally hetero-geneous and conflicted, and asks how an apparatus both produces and destabilizes the norms for gender and sex (1993: 10, 15–16).

In *Gender Trouble* (1990), Judith Butler has developed this critical insight in relation to gendered identity politics in terms of the subversive power of the parodic and the notion of convergence. Butler understands every social-symbolic order to be a regulatory consolidation of power, a Foucauldian apparatus. Such an order is founded by prohibition and maintained by repetition. Here one is

91

able to see how Butler brings Foucault's analytics of power into conversation with Jacques Lacan's emphasis on the social-symbolic constitution of sexual identity.

> Over and against those who argued that sex is a simple question of anatomy, Lacan maintained that sex is a symbolic position that one assumes under threat of punishment, that is, a position one is constrained to assume, where those constraints are operative in the very structure of language and, hence, in the constitutive relations of cultural life.
>
> (Butler 1993: 95–6)

Butler criticizes the false presumption "that to be *constituted* by discourse is to be *determined* by discourse, where determination forecloses the possibility of agency" (1990: 143). This presumption cannot be maintained because, as Irigaray also makes clear, "the subject/object dichotomy, which here belongs to the tradition of Western epistemology, *conditions the very problematic of identity that it seeks to solve*" (144; emphasis added). Thus she asks, "To what extent do identitarian logical systems always require the construction of socially impossible identities to occupy an unnamed, excluded, but presuppositional relation subsequently concealed by the logic itself?" (39). That is, to what extent is otherness posited and enforced by a particular system of identity politics in ways that are logically impossible? What are the inherent problematics of such identities of excluded not-selves within the logic of the system itself? Beginning here, from within the logical system of gendered identity politics (the game having always already begun and the teams having always already been picked), Butler focuses on signifying practices (in writing and elsewhere) that exploit the very problematics inadvertently yet inevitably included within that law and order. For these problematics suggest the possibility of the law's own cultural displacement.

At this point it is not difficult to recognize the affinity between Butler's *Gender Trouble* and Irigaray's deconstructive exegetical analyses of the logic of the same, in which, for example, the woman-as-object is seen as a "bench mark that is ultimately more crucial than the subject" (see above).[2] Once one recognizes that sexual identity within a social-symbolic order is neither biologically nor onto-logically determined, but rather is maintained by regulatory practice, new and subversive questions come to mind. To quote Irigaray again

(1985a: 135): "What if the 'object' started to speak? ... What disaggregation of the subject would that entail?" If discourse is both *productive of* and *produced within* a particular social-symbolic order, what kind of signifying practices in which contexts will break up the pattern of repetition and open that order to its own cultural displacement?

In her exploration of the kinds of signifying practices that might engender such "subversive confusions" within patriarchal identity politics, Butler frequently touches on one point in particular that is suggestive of the problematization of identity in Esther: that is, the *point of convergence*.[3] As she writes,

> the very injunction to be a given gender takes place through discursive routes: to be a good mother, to be a heterosexually desirable object, to be a fit worker, in sum, to signify a multiplicity of guarantees in response to a variety of different demands all at once. *The coexistence or convergence of such discursive injunctions produces the possibility of a complex reconfiguration and redeployment*; it is not a transcendental subject who enables action in the midst of such a convergence. *There is no self that is prior to the convergence or who maintains "integrity" prior to its entrance into this conflicted cultural field. There is only a taking up of the tools where they lie, where the very "taking up" is enabled by the tool lying there.*
>
> (1990: 145; emphasis added)

If there is to be a social-symbolic order of sexual difference, structured as a closed binary network of differences, then particular identities within that order would need to be stabilized and fixed within that network as essentially singular and immutable. Yet it is clear that "agents" within a given political order are never so reducible. The subject within the system is always, like Cixous, a point of convergence – mother, daughter, queen, orphan, exile, Jew, Persian, and so on. And the injunctioned identities that converge at these points are not entirely compatible.

Indeed, the list (mother, daughter, queen, etc.) is always in-exhaustive, incomprehensive, and therefore never totally comprehensible within or according to any particular politics of identity. Butler gives much attention to the "et cetera" at the end, for it endlessly aggravates identity politics (as it aggregates identity) and carries subversive possibilities. As a necessary supplement to any list, the "et cetera" resists closure and stability within the order of the symbolic, and, therefore, will always refuse total determinism of subjects within that order. To conceive of political subjects as points of convergence rather than as integrated wholes opens reflection on the ways particular political subjects always exceed the singular, fixed places allotted them, thus exposing the limits of identity politics and making political transformation possible.

This aspect of Butler's work, which finds resonances in Irigaray and Cixous, proves particularly suggestive for reading Esther. In *Gender Trouble* Butler asks what kind of parodic signifying practices might be subversive of the regulatory practices that form and maintain identity. I would not be surprised if the Bible does not come to mind for very many; indeed, the field of biblical studies appears at first to be far outside the purview of this critical discourse. Yet I would argue that this is not necessarily the case.

Butler, whose work is always in conversation with feminist psychoanalytic reformulations by Luce Irigaray, Jacqueline Rose, and Jane Gallop, among others, assumes a critique of the phallo-centric foundations of the psychoanalytic mythos that guarantees the prohibitionary Law of the Father. Thus Butler, paraphrasing Rose, writes, "the paternal law ought to be understood not as a determin-istic divine will, but as a perpetual bumbler, preparing the ground for the insurrections against him" (1990: 28). From a historical standpoint, many would understand the Hebrew Bible and biblical monotheism as the foundation and guarantee for many forms of Western patriarchal domination, as well as for the gender identities upon which they depend. Some even refer to "biblical prohibition," alluding to both the Bible and Lacan at once. In fact, Lacan himself was intentionally alluding to the biblical legal tradition with his Name of the Father, which plays homophonically in French on "Name" (*Nom*) and "No" (*Non*) as well as "Law" (Greek *Nomos*).[4] Yet is that all the Hebrew Bible admits? Is it univocal, monolithic? Does it offer a reliable guarantee? Is it capable of being the "emblem and agent of the patriarchal system, to shore up the name of the father" (Irigaray 1985b: 67) even as potently as Lacan's Phallus? To say so requires that one ignore, for example, the book of Esther, a text in which the closest thing to a divine guardian of patriarchy is a drunken, pleasure-seeking, highly impressionable king, and in which the ambiguities of identity and the consequent problematics of political orderings based on them are profound and central.

My analysis in the next chapter, which focuses on Esther's "coming-out" party with Haman and the king, will demonstrate the more subversive possibilities of reading biblical literature in conversation with Cixous and Butler.

8

COMING OUT

The law, a chandelier.
This hall of mirrors is the place of the game,
– games of I am.
Palace of straw.
Smoldering fire.

Every day, books fade;
in dreams, they are made.
Surprise lies in wait at the turn.
And risk.

(Jabès 1993: 67)

In this game of I am, of hiding and self-disclosure, surprise is around
every corner, and to survive, one must risk. Outside the palace walls,
a pogrom is heating up. Inside, a drinking party. The Jew is in
sackcloth and ashes, marked for death. The Jew is in royal garments,
favored by the king. Facets of law and order turn and turn again,
reflection upon reflection in this hall of mirrors which is the place of
the game. A deadly serious play. This is the scene of Esther's self-
disclosure of excess, of what cannot fit. This is the scene of her
coming-out.

With the dooming words of Zeresh and the advisors still ringing
through Haman's bewildered head ("you will not overcome ...
but will surely fall"; 6:13), the eunuchs, once again acting as
mediators between the sexes, come to "bring Haman" (*leʰabî' 'et
haman*) to Esther's second drinking party (6:14). The language here
is very close to that used in the king's earlier command to bring
Vashti to his drinking party in chapter 1 (*leʰabî' 'et vashtî*). In
previous episodes, conflicts between Mordecai and Haman have
paralleled the conflict involving Vashti and the king (so that Mordecai

was identified with Vashti, and Haman [like Memucan] with the king). Now, however, the text suggests a different arrangement, by which *Haman* is identified with Vashti in her demise, and Esther (to whose drinking party he is being brought) is identified with the king.

At this second of Esther's drinking parties with Ahasuerus and Haman, Ahasuerus once again bids Esther to make her petition, and this time she does, disclosing a convergence of mutually incompatible identities which thus far has remained closeted, and which cannot fit within the present order of things (7:3–4):

> If I have found favor in your eyes, king, and if it pleases the king, give me my life as my request, and my people as what I seek. For we have been sold, I and my people, to be wiped out, slain, annihilated.[1]

Her revelation begins in typical fashion by piling up stock request phrases, aimed to please: "if I have found favor in your eyes" (cf. 2:15, 17; 5:2, 8; and 8:5), and "if it pleases the king" (cf. 1:19; 3:9; 5:4, 8; 7:3; 8:5; and 9:13). Of course, Esther has been "pleasing" and has "found favor in the eyes of the king" from the beginning. Here, then, she maintains and confirms the king's fixation on her as object, while at the same time beginning to take him in an entirely unexpected direction.

Framed as a petition, her speech is also a means of massive disclosure, for by requesting to be delivered from the Jewish pogrom, she "reveals her people" (cf. 2:10). Moreover, by quoting verbatim from the decree, she makes explicit the identification of herself with the object of obliteration marked by the king and Haman by royal decree (Esther 3). From the king's perspective, this changes everything. It exposes and exploits an unexpected convergence that threatens political upheaval, insofar as Persian national politics has become, based on Haman's identification with the king over against them, totally and violently opposed to the Jews. Here, then, is a surprise act of political agency, involving the deployment of a side to Esther which, up until now, has been hidden from the king's and Haman's sight, and which is incompatible with the irrevocable written law composed by Haman and the king. It is an agency that plays on the convergences of a multiple selfhood.

From chapter 1 up to this point in the narrative, the drinking party in the book of Esther has functioned as a central locus of identification, that is, of making sameness. This functioned primarily with regard to sex in chapter 1. At the end of chapter 2, similarly, it signified a return to "proper" sexual politics as Esther became queen "instead of Vashti." At the end of chapter 3, Haman and the king drinking together signified their identification with one another over against the Jews. And while not a same-sex affair, Esther's first drinking party likewise confirmed Haman's identification with the king, even in relation to her (she threw it for him and the king exclusively; 5:12). In each of these drinking parties, subjects are located and identified together at the very center of the nation. With Esther's disclosure, however, that pattern is shattered. Her revelation, which draws the marginal other into the very center uninvited, puts an end to any such cozy feelings. It introduces the other into the center of the order in a way that exposes and explodes all imagined sameness.

"Who is he," the king asks, "and where is he who is determined to do thus?" (7:5). It appears that the king has not yet put it all together. Or perhaps this is feigned ignorance, aimed at distancing himself from Haman (recall his complicity with Haman in chapter 3). Either way, Esther's response gets him off the hook – whether he realized he was on it or not. Turning against Haman, she declares, "Adversary! Enemy! This evil Haman!" (7:6).

Just as Haman had secured his identity with the king by projecting the Jew as their mutual enemy, and in the process had erased Mordecai's former identification with the king (through his good deed of exposing the eunuch coup; 2:21–3), so here Esther's declaration works to locate the king with herself over against Haman as *their* enemy, and in the process erases the king's own former identification with Haman.[2] By the opening words of her petition in verses 3–4, Esther had disclosed the convergence of her identity as Persian royalty with her identity as the other Jew, marked for oblivion by Persian royal decree, thus embodying both the same and the other simultaneously. With this second declaration, she identifies the decree itself with Haman and dissociates it from the king. At this moment, with this turn, Haman's position as subject of the law along with the king is radically destabilized. So too is the king's, and Esther's. Clearly, Esther's revelation has engendered ambiguity in the relations within the drinking party, as well as within the larger scene of national politics. There is not, however, any guarantee that the political outcome will be in her favor. Despite Esther's planning, this revelation involves great risk, and extremely high stakes (fifty cubits high, in fact).

Immediately following this disclosure, the text describes the two male subjects reeling in the chaos that Esther has engendered. Haman is "panic-stricken[3] *in the presence of the king and queen*" (7:6). For the reader, Haman's terror clearly marks his location *over against* the other two.[4] The terror of Esther has "fallen upon" him. Then the king, whose order is once again destabilized and who is once again "enraged" (*hamah*), rises and storms out of the drinking party and into the garden (7:7). Haman then approaches Esther the queen to "seek his life," just as she has sought her life from the king, "for he saw that evil was destined for him from the king" (7:7). The king then returns from the garden to find Haman "falling over the bed where Esther was" (7:8a), and assumes sexual assault (indicated by the use of *kabash*, "to force" or "subdue"). If the king had not destined evil for Haman yet, he certainly does now. With this coincidence, moreover, it can no longer be clear what decisively seals Haman's fate. Is it the revelation that he seeks to wipe out Esther's people (which would have been the case whether or not Haman had been caught on the bed with her), or is it that he has become too closely identified with the king (wanting not just his robes and horse, but also his wife)? Is the decisive moment in Haman's alienation from the king brought on by his infringement on Esther as Jew or as the king's wife? Or both?

Esther's words leave Haman in a panic and the king in a rage, with Haman's panic contributing to the king's rage and vice-versa. Needless to say, given the narrative pattern of instigation–rage– recommendation–implementation–return of pleasure, by now well established (cf. 1:13–22; 2:2–4; 3:5–15), someone needs to make a recommendation. Enter Harbona, another "one of the eunuchs of the king," who informs the king, "Behold, the very stake which he prepared for Mordecai, whose words pleased the king, is standing at Haman's house, fifty cubits high" (7:9). Harbona's words not only point out a resolution to the king's rage, but also further compound that rage by indicating Haman's violent opposition to Mordecai, whom the king has just remembered to honor.

On previous occasions, the advice given to the king has been explicit with regard to details of procedure (1:16–20; 2:2–4; 6:8–9). This time, however, the king does not need to have it spelled out. He replies, "Hang him on it." The king's order is immediately carried out and, as before, "the rage [*hemah*] of the king settled down" (7:10; cf. 2:1). Thus the episode ends by identifying Haman with the two insurrectory eunuchs, "keepers of the threshold," who were hanged formerly (2:23). Just as in the previous episode (6:1–13) Mordecai came to be dissociated from Bigthan and Teresh, so here Haman comes to be identified with them, at the stake.

None of these reversals would have been possible, however, without Esther's exploitation of identity convergences. More than any other character in the story, she lives under injunctions "to signify a multiplicity of guarantees in response to a variety of different demands all at once" (Butler 1990: 145): to be obedient daughter, to be pleasing wife, to be orphan, to be law-abiding Persian, to be loyal Jew (which demands that she transgress the king's law), to be queen, to be exile, et cetera. Given these multiple injunctions, it is impossible to fix her in a particular social location within an order marked by a particular politics of identity, one based on a system of oppositional differences. At this point in the narrative, moreover, it becomes clear that this impossibility carries with it a subversive use-value. Esther does not choose, as free agent, to play in these fields; rather, she finds herself *signed up* thus. Indeed, even the concealment of "her people" is not, at least initially, a matter of her will but Mordecai's. Yet the "convergence of discursive injunctions" with which this leaves her "produces the possibility of a complex reconfiguration and redeployment" (Butler 1990: 145). Here is this Jewoman's "good and bad luck" (Cixous 1993a: 204).

Esther's strategic coming-out party leaves the king dispositioned also, for he never again quite regains his composure and can barely keep up with the queen's demands (e.g., 9:12). Indeed, in 8:2, after he gives her Haman's household, and after she "revealed what [Mordecai] was to her," Esther "placed Mordecai over [*vatasem . . . 'et-mordecai 'al*] the household of Haman," just as the king had "placed Haman's seat over" (*vayyasem 'et-kis'ô me'al*) all the other royal officials. Significantly, this parallel, along with the fact that the king had just given Mordecai his signet (8:2a) as he had previously given it to Haman (3:10), identifies Mordecai with Haman (as his successor) and Esther with the king. It should be noted in this regard, furthermore, that Esther's disclosure does not signify the *reduction* and *return* of her identity to that of Jew or daughter of Mordecai; on the contrary, the text continues to put some distance between them even in their very titles, which remain "Esther *the queen*" and "Mordecai *the Jew*" throughout the remainder of the story whenever the two are mentioned together (8:7; 9:29, 31).

At this point, moreover, convergences with Vashti, the other woman, also begin to appear, so that her revelation is a coming-out not only of the other Jew but also of the other woman. I have shown (in Chapter 4) how Vashti's and Mordecai's stories converge. There are also traces of Vashti in the one who fills the space she leaves as queen. Remember that it is in fact the king's memory of Vashti (namely her abjectionable act of refusal), not the lack of a queen, that motivates the pageant-search for a replacement (2:1–2; cf. 2:17). The actions of both Vashti and Esther, moreover, are often described in ways that play on the king's actions (and the king often appears disturbed, at times even fearful, in response to the actions of both). As noted already, Vashti is the first acting subject in the narrative other than the king, and she throws a drinking party just as he did. Similarly, in 4:16–17 Esther commands Mordecai in royal fashion, and Mordecai "did everything that she commanded him." In 8:2, furthermore, Esther "placed [Mordecai] over the household of Haman," just as the king had "placed [Haman's seat] over all the chiefs" in 3:1. Thus they possess similar characteristics as royal acting subjects. And of course they share the same status as privileged objects of male ogle and exchange. Both Vashti and Esther are described (at least for a time) as "pleasing to look at" (*tôbat mar'eh*) "in the presence of" (*lipnê*) the king (see, e.g., 1:11; 2:2, 3, 9). In fact they are the only two described in this way.

The fact that they are similar both as subjects and objects, moreover, suggests a third kinship: the ambivalence and excess of their place in the order of things. Neither is reducible to one or the other side of binary ordering principles such as subject/object, self/other, inside/outside, honor/deference, etc., which found the royal sexual-national politics. This irreducibility insinuates instabilities and uncertainties inherent in those binaries. Yet whereas Vashti refuses to come into the king's presence (1:12), Esther by contrast comes frequently into his presence; and each time she makes requests on behalf of her people and against her enemy Haman (see especially 8:3–8; 9:13, 25). In the Vashti/Memucan/Ahasuerus triangle, Memucan was the only one to make suggestions introduced by "if it pleases the king ..." (1:19; cf. 1:21). In the Esther/Haman/Ahasuerus triangle, both Esther and Haman make such requests (3:9; 5:4, 8; 7:3; 8:5–8; 9:13) in a life or death game of hiding and revealing. Vashti refused the status of fixed object. Esther takes the place that had been envisioned for Vashti. Or rather she is *put* there – that is where she finds her start in the story. In the long run, however, she is able to exploit her position and its ambivalences: not fully fixed, not without agency, not fully "in his presence." And as she does so, the male subjects find themselves being led away, someplace other than where they thought they were – finished with the other woman and on the verge of annihilating the other Jew.

COUNTER FIRE

> Writing keeps up the illusion that rescue is near. But fire cannot save us from fire; or cold, from cold; on the contrary, they perpetuate.
>
> (Jabès 1993: 78)

Back at the end of chapter 3, when Haman and the king were drinking together as the city outside reeled in turmoil, "that day" was marked for the total annihilation of all Jews. At the beginning of chapter 8, "that day" finally arrives, but not as people had prepared for it.

> In the twelfth month (that is, the month of Adar), on its thirteenth day, when the king's word and law were to be carried out – the very day that the enemies of the Jews had reserved to gain mastery over them – there was a reversal, when the Jews themselves had mastery over those who hated them.
>
> (9:1)

In ways that parallel the reversal of Mordecai and Haman in relation to the king after Esther's coming-out, everything begins to be turned inside out: what was central is scattered to the margins, and what was scattered in the margins is powerfully consolidated at the center.[5] The subject of the law becomes its hated object, and its hated object becomes its writing subject (9:20, 29–32).

In all this, Jewish identity is shored up and reinforced toward the objective mastery of power, to such an extent that "fear of the Jews" and "fear of Mordecai" falls on people throughout the kingdom (8:17; 9:3). Some commentators (e.g., Horschander 1923: 247; Ringgren 1956: 140; Dommershausen 1968: 110) see in the use of *pahad* ("fear") here a subtle allusion to God (i.e., fear of God), which may then be related to a possible allusion to God's election of the Jews in the prediction by Zeresh and Haman's advisors ("if Mordecai is of Jewish seed . . . you will surely fall"; 6:13). Without denying this possibility, I would insist on the significance of the more direct sense of the people's sudden fear of the other Jew, whom they had formerly hated as oppositional object of their law. Indeed, there has been no God to elect Jews and thereby establish Jewish identity in this story, and so one might also argue that allusions to God only accentuate God's *absence* in the story, and therefore the absence of such religious guarantees. In the present context, such allusions only further the sense that Jewish identity is not entirely self-evident or secure, but is established and defined within political discourse (in this case, by Haman's projection).

In light of this, Est 8:17b is particularly fascinating: "And many of the people of the land were *being Jewish* [*mityahadîm*], for the fear of the Jews had fallen upon them." This is the only instance in the Jewish Bible of a verbal form (Hitpael participle) of the Hebrew word for "Jew." Literally, then, this text reads, "many people of the land *were jewing*." Rashi (in Schwartz and Schwartz 1983: 46), and numerous commentators since, have asserted that the use here signifies *conversion* to Judaism, or perhaps a return to Judaism by non-practicing Jews.[6] Such a view, however, is very problematic. First of all, the Hitpael participle form would more appropriately connote a continuing behavior rather than a single act of conversion or return. Second, what would they be converting to? Given how very little correlation there is in the book between Jewish identity and religious practice, the notion of conversion at this point would appear quite strange. Along with Moore (1971: 82) and Fox (1991b: 105), therefore, I suggest that the verb be understood as a reference to people *behaving* as Jews, suggesting again the performative character of identity – whatever that performance might be in this case. Indeed, the text gives no indication of what kind of behavior would identify one as Jewish. What action? What appearance? What words? After all, Esther herself was able to conceal her identity with the Jews simply by not intentionally disclosing it, and Haman only knew of Mordecai's Jewish identity because Mordecai *had* disclosed it.

Whatever the performance might entail (perhaps one simply begins calling oneself a Jew), Persians everywhere are suddenly "jewing." Earlier, to be identified as Jewish was to be marked for death; now for some Persians it seems to have become a matter of "to jew or die." Then and now, there appears in Esther to be no particular core to Jewish identity. Rather, the book plays – often with deadly seriousness – on Jewish identity as a matter of appearances, disclosures, and withholdings.

On Esther's recommendation, the law is widely published, as were former ones, in an effort to overwrite the earlier law disseminated by Haman and the king (Esther 3). Its basic content is summarized in 8:11, using language similar to the former anti-Jewish decree: "The king permitted the Jews in each and every city to gather and to stand up for their lives,[7] to wipe out, to slaughter, to annihilate any force – any people or province attacking them – [along with] children and women,[8] and to plunder them for goods." And so begins a carnival of terror, as thousands upon thousands of their enemies are massacred – a mirror image of the horrible day that had been expected (9:1). As the killings are enumerated, one cannot help but shudder to imagine the piles of massacred bodies:

> And the Jews struck all their enemies with the blow of the sword. They slaughtered and annihilated. They did to those who hated them as they willed. And in the acropolis of Susa, they slaughtered and annihilated five-hundred men. And they also killed Parshandatha, Dalphon, Aspatha, Poratha, Adalia, Aridatha, Parmashta, Arisai, Aridai, and Vaizatha, the ten sons of Haman, son of Hammedatha, enemy of the Jews. But they did not lay a hand on the plunder.[9]
>
> (9:5–10)
>
> Haman's ten sons were hanged. And the Jews gathered again also on the fourteenth day of the month of Adar, and they slaughtered in Susa three-hundred men, but they did not lay a hand on the plunder.
>
> (9:14b–15)
>
> The rest of the Jews, those in the king's provinces, likewise gathered and fought for their lives. They disposed of their enemies, killing seventy-five thousand of those hating them, but they did not lay a hand on the plunder.
>
> (9:16)

Fox (1991b: 220f.) rightly cautions against imagining that this action by the Jews is altogether identical to that proposed by Haman, as so many Christian interpreters have argued.[10] There is, already in place, an edict aimed at the annihilation of all Jews. While the new edict is intended to overwrite the former one, its success is not certain. The Jews, then, would still need to fight in order to pre-empt implementation of the former law. They are to "stand up for their lives" against "any people or province attacking them" (8:11; cf. 9:16).

At the same time, it must also be recognized that the line which differentiates the Jews from their enemies in these passages remains difficult to draw. Why, for example, does the text describe the slaughter by the Jews in language so close to that of the earlier edict in 3:8? And why is it that in the vignette about the killings in the capital (9:6–15) there is no mention of the Jews being attacked (so as to represent them more clearly in a fight for their lives)? Certainly the text could have avoided any identity confusion whatsoever, and could thus have shored up the differences, simply by using more sharply contrastive language. The fact that the text leaves any room whatsoever to ask whether or not the Jews did differently than their haters intended to do is striking. For that matter, is the text describing a pre-emptive or a defensive strike? Are the Jews killing their "attackers" or their "haters"? Is there a difference? Indeed, the text builds extensive ambiguity into its descriptions of the reversal taking place, even when it could easily have sharpened the distinctions. Consequently, the text raises further questions concerning the problematics of establishing identity-over-against, and plunges readers into a deep ethical maelstrom.

In fact, during and after the revolution, as the other Jew becomes the subject of the death-dealing law rather than its object, things do not appear very different from before. This is even true on the level of sexual politics, for Esther has, after all, turned out to be Mordecai's wisest investment with the king. Indeed, while Esther reaches a pinnacle of public power and authority in chapter 9 (Fox 1991b: 128), the present form of the story's conclusion (its epilogue in Esther 10, which most scholars take to be a late addition; see Clines 1984: 167–8) makes no mention whatsoever of Esther, but only the king and his right-hand man Mordecai. In this respect she winds up resembling Vashti (in absentia). As the narrative concludes, then, there appears to be an effort to "sort things out," to undo the convergences, which have served their purpose but which must no longer remain in play. It is as though the time of crisis is ended, and now everything must return to business as usual.

But is that possible? Can this epilogue undo what the rest of the narrative has done? Such profound questions have been raised about the very identity politics that is now being shored up, that I am left with a knot in my stomach. All the reversals of fortune have been accomplished by exploiting convergences between self and other, us and them. These convergences have not disappeared with this new resolution. The royal legislation written in the wake of Esther's coming-out is aimed at countering the earlier legislation written by Haman and the king, calling for the annihilation of all Jews. But the latter has not erased the former completely, for like a counter fire intended to stop the blaze, it appears to be of like substance. It is writing by the same hand, in the same scripts. It uses like words, and recommends like strategies. For anyone who has read the signs closely, it is impossible to rest securely in the ending. The counter fire may have stopped today's blaze, but the fire will return, perhaps next time from another quarter.

IN CONCLUSION

Final solutions require impossibly clear definitions of the problem. Glorious ends are founded on fantasies of pure origins. Likewise, dislocating beginnings – my own, Vashti's, Esther's, Mordecai's, Haman's – necessarily lead to inconclusive endings.

The book of Esther is about surviving dead ends: living beyond the end determined for those projected as quintessentially not-self, the privileged representatives of divergence, marked as sacrifices for the furtherance of a vision of identity and political homogeneity. Insofar as categories of self and not-self, same and other, are irreducible to pure opposites, insofar as one always exceeds the limits imposed on her by any politics of identity, the end determined for the other – the "final solution" – is impossible. Ultimately, the dream of a final solution, in its desire to eradicate otherness, expresses the impossible desire to purify the self. Impossible, because the problem of the other, construed as "Jewish problem" or otherwise, is also the problem of the self. The one and the other are endlessly entangled, irreducible to either a single whole or an opposition. The royal subject of the law is also, simultaneously, the one marked for oblivion by that law. Abject mingles with subject at a drinking party. The out-of-bounds is closeted within the palace walls.

When taken together, the different threads of interpretation in the preceding chapters lead not so much to a focus on how self and other are defined as to a focus on how such definitions are always unstable and open to subversion. That is to say, this book is less about how lines between us and them get drawn and more about what makes those lines impossible to locate and fix. In my readings of Esther and contemporary theory, I have focused particularly on ambiguities in representations of the other Jew and the other woman, arguing such ambiguities can be used to sabotage the very politics of anti-Judaism and misogyny that rely on these representations of otherness. The following pages bring the different threads of my analysis together in order to develop this argument further.

ADJACENT CLOSETS

My interpretation of the dynamics of hiding and revealing, so key to political transformation in Esther, in relation to the modern trope of closeting and coming out follows Eve Kosofsky Sedgwick's suggestive three-tiered reading of Esther – beginning with Marcel Proust, who, in the "Sodom and Gomorrah" books of *A la recherche du temps perdu*, is preoccupied with Jean Racine's *Esther* (itself a creative recasting of the biblical Esther) as a story of Jewish coming-out (Sedgwick 1990: 72–83). The context for Sedgwick's interpretation is her larger argument that the recent "floating-free" of the metaphors of "the closet" and "coming out" from their gay origins, "now verging on all-purpose phrases for the potent crossing and recrossing of almost any politically charged lines of representation," indicates the centrality of homo/heterosexual definition in Western culture from the late nineteenth century to the present (1990: 71–3). The closet, which is "the defining structure for gay oppression in this century" (71), stands for a series of damaging contradictions and double binds involved in public/private distinctions. Within this argument, and following Proust, Sedgwick examines Jewish identity as a category of ethnicity that is in some ways analogous to homosexual identity, insofar as it can be hidden and disclosed, and insofar as its disclosure has often involved tremendous risk. In this light she reads both Racine's *Esther* and, less directly, the biblical Esther as "enactments of a particular dream or fantasy of coming out" (76).[1]

After drawing this analogy, however, Sedgwick goes on to mark the distance between coming out as Jew in Esther and coming out as homosexual in contemporary culture, stressing how "moments of *Esther*-style avowal must misrepresent the truths of homophobic oppression; these go back to the important differences between Jewish (here I mean Racinian-Jewish) and gay identity and oppression" (1990: 78). It is certainly wise to be circumspect in drawing the analogy, which "more than flirts with sentimentality," and I too must take heed. With that in mind, it is nonetheless worth noting that although Sedgwick peppers her interpretation with passages from the Bible as well as from Racine, the distinctions she draws are between contemporary homophobic oppression and a specifically "*Racinian*" construal of anti-Jewish oppression. I propose that the analogy with the ancient *biblical* Esther may in fact be closer and more suggestive than it is with the late seventeenth-century play by Racine.

All of Sedgwick's points of distinction are pertinent to Racine's *Esther*, but several are not so clear in the biblical text. My reading has raised many complicating questions, for example, about whether "*Esther's avowal occurs within and perpetuates a coherent system of gender subordination*," simply because her start as Queen is intended to restore stability following the crisis of patriarchal identity elicited by Vashti's refusal (Sedgwick 1990: 81, point 7). Is it certain, moreover, that Esther "*knows who her people are and has immediate answerability to them*" (81, point 6)? My reading of Esther's encounter with a desperate and threatening Mordecai (in Esther 4) suggests that their relationship at that point is at least tenuous (as is often the case in the contemporary side of Sedgwick's analogy). With regard to the king in the biblical narrative (i.e., the subject to whom she comes out), on the other hand, Sedgwick's distinctions are valid: first, there is no indication that Ahasuerus might be a closet Jew himself (81, point 5); second, he "*seems to have no definitional involvement with the religious/ethnic identity of Esther*" (80, point 4) – although "seems" is the right word, considering his earlier identification *with* Haman in making the royal decree to annihilate all Jews as the antithesis of Persian national identity; and third, Ahasuerus does not stand to be damaged by Esther's disclosure (80, point 3) – although he does become very deferential to her will afterwards. With regard to the character of Esther, on the other hand, it is too much to say that in the biblical text (as Sedgwick argues is the case in Racine) Esther is confident and in control of other people's knowledge about her, "in contrast to the radical uncertainty closeted gay people are likely to feel about who is in control of information about their sexual identity" (79, point 2). Mordecai certainly could mess things up for her, as is indicated by her agitation with him for showing up in sackcloth and ashes (which she quickly redresses), and by her suspenseful "if if die, I die" (4:16). Even Sedgwick's own comments earlier in the analogy undermine the force of this distinction:

> at this moment the particular operation of suspense around her would be recognizable to any gay person who has inched

toward coming out to a homophobic parent.... That the avowal of her secret identity will have an immense potency is clear, is the premise of the story. All that remains to be seen is whether under its explosive pressure the king's "political" animus against her kind will demolish his "personal" love for her, or vice versa.

(1990: 76)

Sedgwick goes on to comment that both the play and the biblical narrative are "bearable to read in their balance of the holocaustal with the intimate only because one knows how the story will end." Both the fact that Esther was advised to hide her familial and ethnic identity, and the fact that a high-ranking official in Ahasuerus's court hates Jews and finds political support for their extermination, make the risk clear.[2] Esther's coming-out party (7:6ff.) could easily have led to a "morning after" with Esther, rather than Haman, impaled on a stake.

Perhaps the most important distinction Sedgwick makes, however, which I would argue is the least pertinent to the biblical Esther, is that

there is no suggestion that [Jewish] identity might be a debatable, a porous, a mutable fact about her.... The Jewish identity in this play – whatever it may consist of in real life in a given historical context – has a solidity whose very unequivocalness grounds the story of Esther's equivocation and her subsequent self-disclosure. In the processes of gay self-disclosure, by contrast, in a twentieth-century context, questions of authority and evidence can be the first to arise.

(1990: 79, point 1)

My reading of the biblical Esther argues against this supposed "unequivocalness" of Jewish identity. Indeed, as discussed in my last chapter, although Esther's Jewish identity is never questioned after her disclosure, it is also true that there was nothing given or self-evident about it before then. And Mordecai's anxious threat in chapter 4 ("Do not imagine that you will escape with your life ... from all the Jews") indicates that she might have decided *not* to come out. For Esther, and indeed for Mordecai too, Jewish identity can be hidden simply by choosing not to disclose it. That Jewish identity is debatable, porous, mutable in Esther is further evidenced by the comment that people were jewing, whatever that is taken to mean (a conversion ... to what? a performance ... how?). Granted, however deadly serious the story of Esther can be, it is pervaded with the outrageous, the farcical, and at points even the fantastical. Indeed, these are the elements in Esther that above all else distinguish it from narratives of lesbian and gay coming-out in today's homophobic world.

When this distinction by Sedgwick (based on the assumed givenness of Jewish identity) is reconsidered with regard to the biblical Esther, Racine and Proust aside, a significant point of contact comes into focus, namely this: *both in the ancient text of Esther and in modern discourse on homosexuality, the dynamics of hiding and disclosure, closeting and coming out, reflect a historical context of identity ambivalence, with regard to Jewish/non-Jewish identity on the one hand and homo/heterosexual identity on the other.*

Sedgwick's *Epistemology of the Closet* (1990) and *Between Men* (1985) are part of a larger body of scholarship focused on developing a historical context for the emergence of the binary opposition homo/heterosexual (or gay/straight) as a basic means of mapping identities in modern Western European culture.[3] Although today this opposition is often assumed to be self-evident, this growing body of scholarship has shown that its emergence as central to the way we think about identity is a recent development. It owes its prominance to an epistemological shift which took place over the course of the nineteenth century (roughly), from understanding homosexuality as a matter of prohibited same-sex acts to understanding it as a fundamental category of self-definition – something assumed to be a given, despite any ostensible sexual behavior, "so that one's personality structure might mark one as *a homosexual*, even, perhaps, in the absence of any genital activity at all" (Sedgwick 1990: 83). It is in this context of transition and ambivalence with regard to sexual identity – oscillating between act and being – that the modern trope of the closet and coming out has emerged.[4]

Reading Esther through this modern trope of the closet, I suggest that the dynamics of hiding and disclosure in Esther carry a similar significance with regard to Jewish identity in the diaspora; that is, they mark a sense of *ambivalence* with regard to what Jewishness is in the diaspora as opposed to what it was in Judah.

The book of Esther is best understood as historical fiction, or history-like fiction, rather than as historiography *per se*. Yet it is historically significant. For although it is widely agreed that the book has little interest in recording actual historical events from the

Persian period or after (see, e.g., Berg 1979: 1–30; 1980; Moore 1971: xxxiv–liii; cf. Clines 1991: 129–36), it is nonetheless set within the early Jewish diaspora (fifth century BCE), and, as a "socially symbolic act" (Jameson's phrase [1981]), it provides insights into Jewish political self-perception in that context. This is not to suggest that it represents diaspora Judaism as a whole, for there has never been any such homogeneous cultural entity as "diaspora Judaism," as the name itself implies. To the contrary, as a site of Jewish self-interrogation, and therefore as a site for interrogating traditional projections of that self's other as well, the book of Esther reflects a context in which the traditional means of self-construal have lost their meaning. In Esther the Jew's link with historical roots is also the point of rupture from those roots: the exile, being carried off (see Esther 2:6). In Daniel, another biblical narrative of the Jewish diaspora, that rupture is mended by religious adherence and loyalty to the God of Judaism. But one searches in vain for anything of the sort in Esther. Indeed, it is *Haman the Jew-hater* who conjures the sharpest definition of Jewish identity in diaspora, projecting an image of the Jew as Persian national identity's quintessential negative image, the one divergence in an otherwise homogeneous, harmonious whole (Esther 3:8). Yet Haman knows that Mordecai is Jewish not because of his divergent behavior, but because Mordecai reveals himself as Jewish. Remember that Jewish identity in Esther is hidden simply by avoiding intentional disclosure. How could such quint-essential otherness be so easily hidden? In Esther, operations of hiding and disclosure highlight the ambivalence of being Jewish in dispersion, out of Judah, the land in which Jewishness had tradition-ally been acted out.

CONVERGENCES

Esther's coming-out is, I have argued, a disclosure of identity convergences that are mutually incompatible, "socially impossible," as Judith Butler (1990: 39) puts it, insofar as their disclosure makes clear that "Esther" exceeds any single location within the social order that has been established. Another kind of convergence that has been important to my reading of Esther is the convergence of the other woman Vashti and the other Jew Mordecai. Unlike the socially impossible convergences on Esther, this convergence is developed primarily through narrative parallels. To summarize briefly: in Est 1:16–22, Vashti's refusal to be reduced to an object leads to a reinscription of the king's law of sexual politics, in opposition over against her, according to the logic of the same, with Memucan speaking for "us"; in Est 3:8–15, a strikingly similar process takes place concerning ethnic identity politics, over against the "one people who diverge," the Jews, established as the quintessential not-selves in Haman's discourse with the king. Thus the other Jew, like the other woman, comes to be marked for oblivion according to the same logic, which is logic of the same. In the first instance this process identifies Memucan with the king and in the second it identifies Haman with the king. Remarkably, both in chapter 3 and again in chapter 5, Mordecai, as well as all Jews (by identification with him), come to be identified textually with Vashti. Thus the other woman, outlaw of phallocratic sexual politics, marked for oblivion, converges with the other Jew, outlaw of ethnic identity politics, also marked for oblivion. As is clear from my exegetical analysis of chapters 1, 3, and 5, this is accomplished both by particular intertextual relations (words, phrases, etc.) and by overall patterns (the other's refusal; the subject's rage; a recommendation; its implementation; and the return of the subject's pleasure/abatement of rage).

This convergence of Mordecai and Vashti suggests, moreover, a sort of "feminization" of Mordecai as ethnic other, and a "Judaiz-ation" of Vashti as gendered other, which is strikingly similar to the feminization of Jews throughout much of European history. Sander Gilman (1991: esp. 63–76, 133–7, 207) and Marjorie Garber (1992: 224–9), among others, have shown how European culture has often marked off the Jewish man from legitimated European male sexual identity by linking him to the "effeminate," as well as the "de-generate" (Garber 1992: 224; see also Boyarin 1997). Thus, for example, Jewish males have been depicted as menstruating; in the nineteenth century, similarly, a Jewish man's manner of speech, characterized in terms of the Jewish "break in the voice," was identified with femininity as well as homosexuality; this, in turn, might be related to circumcision, perceived as a little castration (Garber 1992: 226–9). (In this regard, Mordecai's identification with the eunuchs is suggestive as well; see below.) In other cases, Jewish men, especially lenders, have been identified with women who were prostitutes, so that the two groups, each integral to the state economy and each at the same time representing otherness in relation to the state's universal subject, are marked for social degradation and persecution.

In a recent study, Daniel Boyarin has developed this discussion in relation to Pauline and post-Pauline New Testament discourse, arguing that allegorical interpretation of Scripture, understood to be a continuation of Hellenic valuing of the One over the many, and a universalizing "global discourse on the meaning of language and the human body and especially on human difference" (1994: 17), is largely responsible for the emergence (and convergence) of misogyny and anti-Judaism in the West. "The desire for univocity manifested by allegoresis and frustrated by the material, embodied signifier is the same Hellenic search for univocity which the Universal Subject disembodies forth and which is frustrated by women and Jews as the embodied signifiers of difference" (Boyarin 1994: 17).

Garber, Gilman, and Boyarin, among others, show how this strategy of converging femininity with Jewishness has been aimed at marking off the not-self, in order to shore up a universal masculine identity (unambiguous, non-ethnic, untainted by the feminine). A similar dynamic of identity politics is operative in the book of Esther, in which, as I have shown, the other woman Vashti and the other Jew Mordecai, along with the collective identities represented by them, are marked off in order to shore up certain identities in the realms of both sexual and ethnic identity politics.

There is, however, also a major difference between the strategies for feminizing Jewish males as manifested in European history (Gilman, Garber) and in the Hellenic/allegorical origins of misogyny and anti-Judaism (Boyarin) on the one hand, and the narrative strategy of Mordecai's feminization in the book of Esther on the other. The difference has primarily to do with point of view and the book's use of parody in its representations of public power (i.e., the king and his advisors who, through writing laws, seek to mark off these not-selves). Insofar as the text encourages identification of the reader *with* the other woman *and* the other Jew, particularly through various strategies of parody against the ostensible power possessed by the subjects of the law who mark them for oblivion, its feminization of the other Jew and its Judaization of the other woman are positively charged. As an antecedent to the feminization of Jews in Greco-Roman and European history, then, the book of Esther is also far more critically aware of the profound ambiguities inherent in identity politics, and of the potentially incendiary openings to political subversion introduced by the convergence of the two. Simply put, this feminization in Esther is not intended as a cut-down; rather, it presents a solidarity of not-selves.

Ironically, moreover, this convergence of Vashti with Mordecai, which I have suggested undermines formalist assumptions in common readings of Esther (which bracket or frame off Vashti's story from the "main" body of the story), is established on *formal* grounds, insofar as it relies on the identification of parallel narrative sequences involving like characters and like identity-political conflicts. Rather than isolating Vashti and Mordecai from one another as types within two discrete narrative units, I am suggesting that in Esther this narrative strategy allows Vashti's resistance and ultimate exscription to trace itself through the rest of the book. This, in turn, plays an important role in bringing issues of gender identity into closer convergence with issues of Jewish identity, which aggravates the problematics inherent in political strategies based on the definition of either.

Mordecai is a site for other convergences as well. For example, he is affiliated, at least for a time, with the two insurrectory eunuchs, Bigthan and Teresh, "keepers of the threshold" (2:21–3; cf. 6:14), and, relatedly, with locales of ambiguity and marginality outside the palace walls. Ambiguous with regard to their own sexual identity within the binary oppositional structure of sexual difference,[5] the eunuchs in Esther occupy the space between as a kind of "third sex." They are "keepers of the threshold," limin-straddlers, transversing and transgressing the line of definition between the sexes. In the sexual politics of the story, the threshold represents non-status, a no-place, neither here nor there, neither this nor that, neither same nor opposite. As is suggested by the planned coup of Bigthan and Teresh, moreover, there is a certain kind of power for subversion in this region that is not readily accessible from the throne room – that is, unless it is revealed by someone else, as Mordecai does through Esther in 2:21–2.

Mordecai himself appears to have one foot on the threshold with Bigthan and Teresh and the other eunuchs, and one foot in the throne room with Esther. Moreover, although Mordecai is never actually called a eunuch (*sarîs*), and although it is pointless to revive age-old arguments about Nehemiah in order to suggest that Mordecai too may have been an actual eunuch, there can be no question that Mordecai's own sexual identity is ambiguous, insofar as he is unmarried and has no children of his own – an uncommon position for a male subject in the Hebrew Bible. This ambiguity, along with the convergence of his story with Vashti's, and along with his access to the realm of the eunuchs (and even to the planned subversion by two of them), further compounds and complicates the identity convergences on Mordecai – convergences that remain for the reader even after they have been ruled out by the king. Beginning with the king's bout with insomnia in chapter 6, his identification with the king is strengthened, as is his dis-identification from Bigthan and Teresh and the margins as he publicly transvests as the king (in his clothes, on his horse, wearing a royal crown) by the king's command. From the king's perspective this new identification distances him from the insurrectory eunuchs (whose coup he exposed). For the reader, however, the old identity convergences do not disappear, but loom large as the story moves into reverse toward its horrific denouement.

Finally, there are convergences between Mordecai and Haman, who are, in a sense, shadows of one another.[6] Indeed, as Magonet astutely suggests (1980), Haman's projection of Mordecai and all Jews over against Persian identity masks Haman's own identity ambivalence, as outsider like Mordecai.[7] Thus in Esther, anti-Judaism is represented as a form of (self-)projection, by which the Jew-hater pushes all otherness onto the Jews and marks them for death – a problematically-founded final solution as self-purification that is strikingly similar to the classic analysis of Fascist anti-Semitism by Adorno and Horkheimer, written during World War II.[8]

> The Jews ... are branded as absolute evil by those who are absolutely evil, and are now in fact the chosen race. Whereas there is no longer any need for economic domination, the Jews are marked out as the absolute object of domination pure and simple. . . . The portrait of the Jews that the nationalists offer to the world is in fact their own self-portrait.
>
> (Adorno and Horkheimer 1991:168)

Reading Esther can open windows onto the strategies and mechanisms for projecting visions of negativity, abjection, divergence, otherness (construed along lines of ethnicity as well as gender), and in the process can expose ambivalences and insecurities in the ones running the projector.

GOD NEVER COMES OUT

Where is Esther indicated in the Torah? "And I will surely hide ['astîr] my face."

(Talmud Hullin 139b)

אסתר: "I am hiding," "I will hide." Rabbinic tradition suggests reading Esther as a book of *divine* hiding. Thus, for example, the Talmud passage quoted above finds in Esther's name an allusion to Deuteronomy 31:18, where God declares, "I will surely hide [*haster 'astîr*] my face/presence from them."[9] But would such an intertextual relation necessarily suggest the assurance of *veiled presence*, as so many modern commentators wish? Or does it rather assure *divine unavailability*? Indeed, the sense in Deuteronomy 31 is that of abandonment by God; and that abandonment is construed as punishment for the people's refusal to act (more literally, to walk) according to God's commands. In Deuteronomy, which is set as a sermon from Moses on the verge of entering the promised land, that punishment is imagined first and foremost as exile – loss of land, dislocation, signifying the literal and figural *ungrounding* of the Jewish people and Jewish identity in dispersion. Moreover, insofar as there is a foundational relation between God, as divine speaking subject of election, of the Torah, of return, on the one hand, and the human subject in biblical literature on the other, what would be the significance of God hiding? Can the foundation and guarantor of identity for the biblical subject be hidden? If so, what does that suggest about the stability of identity? The issue of God's hiding in/from the book of Esther, no matter how construed, does not solve the problem of theological ungroundedness; to the contrary, it contributes to the sense of dislocation that a diaspora context might introduce to traditional conceptions of both ethnic and gender identity.

The book of Esther is in subtle dialogue with many other biblical texts, including the Joseph narratives, Samuel, and Deuteronomy, as well as, to some extent, wisdom literature (Talmon 1963; but see Crenshaw 1976) and the Exodus/Passover traditions (Gerleman 1966; Fewell 1992). This fact changes the dimensions of the book dramatically, because it contextualizes Esther within the dialogical space of canonical Scripture. Yet this canonical context only makes its lack of reference to divine presence or Jewish religious practice all the more striking.[10] It is certainly ironic that the biblical text most intensely and intentionally focused on hatred and violence toward Jews makes no reference whatsoever to the biblical God, and only slight reference, if any, to Jewish religious practice.[11] Indeed, within an intratextual field such as Esther's, it would require a concerted effort to avoid such references.

In Esther, there is no climactic revelation, no divine judgment day, no coming-out for God.[12] In the absence of God, King Ahasuerus is a sort of trick mirror, reflecting that absence in his own vacuousness. His void mimics the void of divine power/presence/authority in the story world. He is a black hole at the center of the concentric rings of public power, a dangerous lack into which various parties (Memucan, Haman, certain eunuchs, Esther, Mordecai) interject their own interests through the discourse of pleasing ("if it pleases the king . . ."). Everyone works through him, but he has no plans of his own. He is profoundly superficial, the only purposes he initiates being those of display at drinking parties: to display his riches and greatness and to display his good-looking wife Vashti (both in chapter 1). As the absence at the center of public power, he is, most literally, *farced*: stuffed with the interests and objectives of those around him. In fact, through the entire book of Esther, the king never once denies a proposal or request. He is the antithesis of divine prohibitionary power – the Law/No of the Father – so often imagined by scholars as what puts the "biblical" in biblical literature.

This farcical representation of royal power in Esther envisions a political domain that is highly unstable and open to transformation, as is clear from the success of every proposal made in the story (from Memucan in chapter 1, from the advisors in chapter 2, from Haman in chapters 3 and 5, from Esther in chapters 5 and 7–9, and so on). Yet there is another side to the sense of political possibility opened up by this representation of power: no transformation can ever be guaranteed or fixed, even for a moment. The vacuous king, as the center of public power and policy, offers no grounding; indeed, it is his quicksand-like character that opens possibilities for power shifts in the first place. And certainly no writing is able to secure each new order as it emerges either, for each successive written publication of law, always pretending irrevocability and universality, is inevitably followed by another that writes over or around it.

One is inclined to ask, What kind of Scripture is this? God hiding, and a royal buffoon filling the space of divine retreat, no sign of religion or religious practice, no sacred space, Mount Sinai lost behind smoke and ashes, the Law of the Father illegible: What does this have to do with anything we commonly assume to be "biblical"? Everything. But not as an affirmation of those assumptions. Esther is present within the biblical canon as a kind of *fracture*, a fissure in the divinely ordained order established elsewhere, opened by the experience of exile and diaspora. Indeed, I suggest that it be understood, like Job, Qohelet (Ecclesiastes), and other biblical texts, as an *interrogation* of biblical authority from within – a biblical self-interrogation.[13] Luther wished Esther did not exist, and many others since have had the same wish. Why? Because it does not fit with what they believe to be "biblical." I suggest that this is precisely why it must be embraced: because it allows us to think the limits of common, simplistic assumptions about "the biblical," and even about religious literature in general, which pervade intellectual discourse today.

WRITING DISPERSION

> How to tell of our bonds? By referring to exile, perhaps, which is the center, the oil spot.
>
> (Jabès 1993: 78)

Esther is about identity in dispersion. It marks off a space of dislocation in which Jewishness may be more a product of projection by one's enemies than a matter of self-definition.

Because of its significance as historical fiction, scholars classify Esther, along with the book of Daniel and other non-canonical texts, as a *diaspora novella*, representing the predicaments and aspirations of Jews in diaspora. As such, it not only demonstrates the possibility of Jews attaining high standing in the royal court, but also suggests how one with such opportunities ought to conduct oneself *vis-à-vis* one's Judaism or gender (see especially Humphreys 1973; and White 1989). Such generic identification and analysis has provided important insights into the book's importance as Scripture, both in terms of its use-value for Jews in diaspora and in terms of its relation to other biblical literature (especially Daniel, and the Joseph narratives in Genesis 37–50; see Berg 1979; and cf. Fewell 1992). Yet, at the same time, this interest has held the focus of scholars too strictly on the age-old practice of evaluating characters in terms of their moral worth as models. Without denying the importance of these insights altogether, my own focus on issues of diaspora identity in Esther moves critical inquiry in a very different direction. I read Esther as a literature of identity crisis, brought about initially by exile and dispersion, and accentuated by an identity politics that frames this scattered people as the one problematic divergence, and then explores the possibilities of transformation produced by that crisis. Jewish identity in diaspora is displaced, as Judah has been carried away, ungrounded, dispersed, and to some degree alienated from a God who remains, at best, hidden. The biblical subject has been disoriented, decentered, and experiences identity as not-self in relation to the dominant social-symbolic order. In this sense, diaspora identity is profoundly para-doxical, close to Jabès's sense of exile as both bonding point and oil spot. This understanding also makes possible identification with an insurrectory "foreign" (i.e., non-Jewish) woman, the patriarchal subject's ultimate not-self, the privileged representative of danger and threat to identity, elsewhere in biblical literature.[14]

Such identifications with otherness in the Jewish diaspora lead to a major disaggregation of the subject who is, in Esther, put on trial by exile and diaspora, with ever-increasing stakes under the abjecting laws of the king and his advisors. This dynamic of identity politics, in turn, leads in Esther to a sharpened awareness, both of the problematic assumptions grounding gender and ethnic identity, and of the deconstructive, transformative possibilities opened up by these problematics.

At this point, related issues of political agency emerge yet again, and deserve further discussion. Contemporary assumptions about political agency, based (often unawares) in modern philosophical conceptions of the subject of history, require clear and singular identity, so that the subject can, with integrity, take a solid stand – a "clear position" – on the political playing-field. The book of Esther, on the other hand, explores the possibilities of political subversion and transformation produced by the problematic limits and ambi-valences of identity – the non-viability of complete integrity. Survival in the book of Esther relies precisely on the *impossibility*, and therefore the *surpassibility*, of the limits imposed on identity accord-ing to the logic of the same. Within Esther, as I have shown, this political transformation takes place especially by way of socially impossible (mutually incompatible) identity convergences. Butler's comments at the conclusion of *Gender Trouble* (1990: 147) are particularly suggestive with regard to my analysis of political agency in Esther:

> Paradoxically, the reconceptualization of identity as an *effect*, that is, as *produced* and *generated*, opens up possibilities of "agency" that are insidiously foreclosed by positions that take identity categories as foundational and fixed. . . . Construction is not opposed to agency; it is the necessary scene of agency, the very terms in which agency is articulated and becomes culturally intelligible.

Esther is not about self-definition, but about being defined over against a self with whom one is refused identification. It is not about the subject's articulation of a social-symbolic order, as might be argued with regard to other biblical texts in, for example, Torah (see, e.g., Kristeva 1982: 90–112) or Proverbs (see, e.g., Newsom 1989). Rather, it is about finding oneself already "signed up without having begun to play" (Irigaray 1985a: 22). It is a story about hatred of the other from the other's point of view.

This issue of the relation between identity and political agency in diaspora has always carried an undercurrent of interest in Esther studies, especially with regard to perennial questions of free will versus determinism. Fox (1991b: 249–50) rightly affirms that the scroll assumes both, although he focuses on how Haman's "best laid plans" are undermined by divine providential control over history, as he sees it evidenced subtly in the reference to "another place" (4:14) and in the prediction of Haman's wife and advisors ("If Mordecai ... is of Jewish seed, ... you ... will surely fall before him"). Fox writes, "It never really was possible that the Jews would be destroyed. ... Jewish existence was truly in danger, yet Jewish victory somehow was, and always will be, written into the script" (1991b: 250). My analysis, which does not offer such positive theological affirmation, turns Fox's insight in another direction, focusing on the agency not of Haman, but of Esther, and on the determinisms not of God, but of Haman via the king and royal power. In this light, it is not agency that is frustrated by a determined end, but the reverse. To be constructed within a particular social-symbolic order is not to be absolutely determined by it.[15] Hope emerges here, on political grounds, in the affirmation not that history is ultimately determined, but that it can never be determined and is always open to subversion, precisely because it cannot contain and control otherness. Otherness is always infiltrating sameness, and vice-versa.

In Esther, no wholehearted resolve or final solution can be certain, not even the tidy reversal of fortune for the Jews in the latter chapters. The farcical representations of royal power throughout the book cannot be dismissed or defaced simply because that power is now, for the time being, in the hands of Jews. The subversive possibilities opened by the book's representation of public power cannot be undone simply because that power has gone through a new Jewish consolidation. In this sense, the fairy-tale settlement in chapter 10, at which point Esther disappears while Mordecai rises to be the king's right-hand man, is no more final than the end of chapter 3 depicting Haman and the king drinking together while the city outside the palace walls is thrown into pandemonium. The text leaves unsettled many questions and ambiguities concerning the emerging powerful, centralized Jewish identity at the end of the book, even while it relates the Jewish people's reversal, reconsolidation, and shoring up of power/identity. How can this final shoring-up ever hold? How can this ending be believable except as a carnival dream which lasts only as long as one sleeps, until another rustling in the night, between bouts of insomnia and terror?

Here again Esther appears to be haunted, paradoxically, by more recent legacies of anti-Judaism that it could never fully have anticipated. As Fox puts it, "other Hamans are always waiting to revive the attempt. . . . The Haman legend has pursued us through history as an ongoing potential" (1991b: 12). A story from the Talmud captures the tension well:

> Rabbah and R. Zera joined together in a Purim feast. They became mellow [i.e., with wine], and Rabbah arose and cut R. Zera's throat. On the next day he prayed on his behalf and revived him. Next year he said, Will your honor come and we will have the Purim feast together? He replied: A miracle does not take place on every occasion.
>
> (Talmud Megillah 7b)

Today, in the aftermath of the Holocaust, the humor of this story echoes more ominously in R. Zera's punchline. Perhaps Elie Wiesel's tragic "Purimschpiel within a Purimschpiel," *The Trial of God*, understands Esther's strange mix of carnivalesque and unfulfilled horror best of all. In it, the minstrel Avrémel, who a little earlier had been hoping for a circus with "bears that dance like people who dance like bears" (1979: 119), says "I imagine Purim without the miracle of Purim. And I know everything" (151). In its impossible ending/impossibility of an ending, the book of Esther anticipates Avrémel's shudder of imagining.

PURIMSCHPIEL

This book did not begin with a party, but it will end with one – Purim, a party that is both profoundly farcical and profoundly haunted.

The book of Esther plays on the borderlines between the ostensible and the inostensible: between overt power and covert power,
between the public and the private, between identity and difference,
between sameness and otherness, between the determined and the
accidental, between disclosure and hiding. This is also where Purim
plays. As carnival performance, Purim is a communal embodiment
of the book *par excellence*, subverting authority, inebriating sobriety,
blurring the lines between self and other, and laughing in the face of
chillingly real historical possibilities.

Esther's own coming-out is particularly suggestive in relation to
the masquerades, and especially the transvestings, common at Purim
celebrations. As I argued in the previous chapter, when Esther came
out, she did not simply and finally reveal her "true" identity. Rather,
she revealed her *manyness*, her *excessiveness* – an "I" with no single,
integrating center, a locus of convergences that are often in tension
with one another in ways that both put her in danger and carry
potential for political subversion. Her revelation of an "I" that could
not "be reduced to one," to borrow Irigaray's phrase, turned the
world inside out and upside down, but it could just as easily have led
to her execution, along with all the Jews of Persia. Her manyness is
both dangerous and potentially subversive precisely because it makes
clear that she, like Mordecai and the others in the story, plays acrosss
boundaries of self/other definition: between Persian/Jew, man/
woman, inside/outside, active/passive, subject/object, author of
annihilation/marked for annihilation.

A similar dynamic can be seen at work in Purim. Purim expresses
its closeness to the text of Esther's play on the borderlines of
self/other definition through its masquerades, and especially through
masquerades that involve *transvesting*, that is, masquerades in which
one crosses over a boundary line between identities that are culturally conceived as opposites (transvesting = "dressing across").[16] It is
not uncommon, for example, for contemporary Purim plays to be
done in drag, with women playing the male parts and men playing
the female parts. Moreover, celebrants of Purim often dress as the
quintessential Jew-hater, Haman. This kind of cross-dressing brings
to mind the command in the Talmud, discussed above, to get so
drunk that one cannot tell the difference between Mordecai and
Haman. Indeed, I would argue that this ancient Talmudic command
fosters a sort of *transvision*, a seeing cross-wise. That is, it calls one
to envision the world in ways that blur culturally conceived boundaries between us and them.

In Purim, one is invited into a live, communal engagement with the book of Esther that renders problematic the lines between self and other which we so often assume to be self-evident. Purim plays on the preposterousness of defining one's self over against an other. As such, Purim, like the text from which it receives its life, explores the possibilities for political transformation and subversion opened by the problematic limits and ambiguities of identity. Clearly, much of the transvesting in contemporary Purim celebrations goes beyond the identity-crossings that we have seen in the book of Esther (there are no drag queens in this ancient text). Purim is not simply a reiteration of Esther. Rather, it is a *survival* of Esther. That is, Purim lives beyond Esther, supplementing it in ways that make it meaningful in today's world. Through the masking and the trans-vesting of Purim, one may recognize ways that one's own self is inextricably mixed with otherness, and otherness with one's self. Purim invites us to recognize, and even to celebrate, the otherness within us that we so often try to repress or hide. Purim is, in this sense, a coming-out party. Purim crosses boundaries, and invites others to do the same.

NOTES

PREFACE

1 Throughout this book I use the term "anti-Judaism" rather than "anti-Semitism" because the latter refers more properly to hatred of Jews in Western culture, especially since the nineteenth century (see Gilman 1991: 5, 125–6). Although my work is certainly pervaded by issues of modern Western anti-Semitism, I do not consider this to be the appropriate term for describing Jew-hatred in the ancient text of Esther.
2 For excellent analyses of the Greek versions of Esther (the Septuagint and the Alpha Text) in relation to the Masoretic text of Esther, see especially Michael V. Fox (1991a) and David J. A. Clines (1984). For a feminist analysis that compares the beginning of the Masoretic text to the beginnings of the two Greek versions, see Beal (1995: 107–10).

INTRODUCTION: DISLOCATING BEGINNINGS

1 This is possible with the unpointed Hebrew text of her name. See the discussion in the Conclusion.
2 On survival as over-living or living-beyond (a notion that I play on at several points in this book), see especially Derrida (1991: 3–34), Detweiler (1991: 239–55), and Linafelt (1995: 45–61).
3 I focus on this passage from Luther's *Table Talk* because it in particular has had such a significant impact on subsequent biblical interpretation, especially among Protestant scholars. For fuller research and interpretation on Luther's view of the book of Esther throughout his work, see Bardtke (1964: 81–5; cf. 1965–6: 117–18).
4 On a less general level, neo-orthodox dialectical thinking and a Hegelian dialectics of history are significantly different, especially with regard to the neo-orthodox insistence on the absolute otherness of God. In Hegel, God is, in a sense, reduced to the Concept (*der Begriff*) itself, which is the condition of all thought and the ground of being; the March of History, then, is construed as human progress toward realization and

125

full embodiment of the Concept, the "achievement of transparent self-consciousness" (Taylor 1994: 597), which is, at the same time, the full presence of God. On the theological dimensions of Hegel, see especially Taylor (1994: 592–610) and Vattimo (1992: 41).

1 WRITING OUT, I

1 Ahasuerus is mentioned by name three times in the opening three verses, with emphasis placed on his secure control over a vast dominion. The two verbs immediately identified with this subject are the participle *hammolek* ("who reigned") and the infinitive *k^{e}shebet* ("when he rested" or "sat"), and the territory governed by the first verb ("from India to Ethiopia, 127 provinces") covers virtually all of the known world at the time (cf. Talmud Megilla 11b). The name Ahasuerus can be positively identified with Xerxes I, son of Darius, who reigned over the Persian empire from 485 to 465 BCE (see Paton 1908a: 51–4; Fox 1991b: 14). However, other than the references in these first two verses, there are very few details in MT Esther which would be of use for a historical reconstruction, or for locating the book's earliest historical context other than as the Jewish diaspora in Persia. The phrases "and it was in the days" (v. 1) and "in those days" (v. 2) set the story in the legendary past.
2 The text of 1:8 concerning the king's command for all to drink has troubled translators. The basic sense, as I understand it, seems to be that everyone was required to have a good time. The readings of Josephus (*Antiquities* XI.188) and others, who argue that all were required to take a drink whenever the king did, are imaginative but unconvincing. It is important for this statement to agree with the second half of the verse, in which the king *orders* everyone to do *as he wishes*. Thus I translate the verse as follows: "The drinking was by law without constraint, for thus the king ordered all officials in his house: to do as each one willed."
3 There is no straightforward way to treat this elliptical Hebrew text (from *hêl* to *l^{e}panayw*). Some (e.g., Moore 1971: 5) have suggested that *w^{e}sarê* be inserted before *hêl* (thus, "[and the chiefs of] the army of Persia and Media ... were in his presence"). I propose that the text be translated as it stands, taking *hêl* not as "army" but rather as "the might of" or "the strength of." The sense here is that all the major representatives of the Persian power structure are present with the king. Cf. the similar use in 8:11.
4 As others have noted (e.g., Fox 1991b: 16–17, following Ibn Ezra; and Hans Striedl 1937: 86), the description of the decor and the drinking in verses 6–7 involves a peculiar "one-membral" sort of sentence structure. Fox (1991b: 16) comments, "The exclamatory listing creates a mass of images that overwhelm the sensory imagination and suggest both a sybaritic delight in opulence and an awareness of its excess."
5 *y^{e}qar*, "honor," occurs ten times in the book of Esther (1:4, 20; 6:3, 6 [twice], 7, 9 [twice], 11; and 8:16) – more than anywhere else in the Hebrew Bible. The next most frequent usage is in the Aramaic material of Daniel (2:6, 37; 4:27, 33; 5:18, 20; 7:14), where it is likewise best

understood in terms of honor. Throughout Esther, it is clear, as it is in anthropological studies (esp. Pitt-Rivers 1977; Peristiany and Pitt-Rivers 1992), that honor is closely related to social power, particularly male dominance. On the integral relationship between "patriarchal" domination and socio-economic hierarchies of power more generally, see especially the anthropological studies of John Davis (1977) and Jane Schneider (1971: 1–24). See also, most recently, Lillian R. Klein (1995: 149–75).

6 In fact, many readers, especially in rabbinic interpretive tradition, have treated this scant notice of Queen Vashti's party and her pointed but unexplained refusal as large gaps in the narrative, and have gone about the business of trying to fill them. Some imaginative occupations of this textual gap have shown very high regard for the queen. See, e.g., Targum Sheni, where the queen lectures the king about her higher nobility, and scolds him for suggesting that she be degraded by displaying herself naked before a party of drunken men. Others have rendered her abominable. Rashi's commentary (in Schwartz and Schwartz 1983), for example, cites a rabbinic tradition claiming that, because she used to strip Jewish girls naked and do work with them on the Sabbath, she was punished by being stripped naked on the Sabbath herself (cf. Megilla 12b). This kind of misogynous treatment of a foreign woman who is perceived as threatening recalls biblical and extrabiblical traditions concerning Jezebel, among others. It should be noted, however, that these same traditions often view Ahasuerus, too, as a profaner (e.g., Megilla 12a; Panim Aherim 58; Abba Gorion 9; in Ginzberg 1941).

7 At the same time, she is called to help locate the king at the center of the center, since the one they all love to look at is *his*.

8 I am reading the *Qere* to agree with verse 14.

9 Note that *qatsap* ("to be wrathful," "to foment") was used in verse 12 to describe the king's reaction to the queen's refusal. Given this connection, and its indefinite subject here, it may read as a reference to the wrath of the *chiefs* in reaction to the insurrectional behavior of their women. Thus, just as the king was enraged at his woman's transgression, so will the chiefs be enraged at the behavior of their women.

10 It is intriguing in this regard that some rabbinic tradition understood her refusal to be due to the fact that "leprosy had broken out on her" (noted in Rashi's commentary on 1:12 [in Schwartz and Schwartz 1983]).

11 I am thankful to Jean-François Lyotard for sharing his reflections on Nancy's notion of exscription in relation to biblical texts, especially with regard to the dynamic of sacrifice as the marking of something to be passed over, beyond a limit or threshold, in order to maintain the order within.

12 Memucan, too, will not return after chapter 1. It is as if his duty has been accomplished. Insofar as he is the most obvious spokesman for the king's patriarchy, the gender-based struggle itself, as well as Vashti, seems to fade into the background as the more obvious struggle for Jewish deliverance begins to develop. Yet, insofar as there are traces of Vashti in Esther, and Memucan in Haman, the gender-based struggle and the "gender trouble" insinuated in Esther 1 trace themselves into the

subsequent story. I discuss the narrative's identification of Memucan
with Haman again in my concluding chapter.

13 In fact 2:4b is identical to 1:21, except that here he "did thus," whereas
in 1:21 he "did the word of Memucan." In both cases, his pleasure is
linked with doing, word for word, what is recommended by another
with regard to the problem of Vashti.

14 Note that the verb is also frequently used in Leviticus in reference to
sacrifice and the Levitical portion, as well as to the Levitical cities, which
are called by the nominal form of the same root. Cf. the "separate place"
(*haggizrah*) described in Ezekiel 41–2.

15 The use of jussive forms in the recommendation is identical to Memucan's
use in 1:16–20, thus creating another link between this episode and the
previous one. Unlike the earlier high officials ("wise ones") "who
know the law" (1:14), however, the advisors here are simply called
"servants of the king ... who serve him" (*mᵉshartaw*), like the seven
eunuchs who were to bring Vashti to him (also described as *hamshartîm*,
"those serving," in 1:10).

16 I am emending to *heggai*. See also 2:8, where the same character
(into whose hands the virgins are delivered) is called by this name.
Cf. 8:14–15 and LXX.

17 *tamrûq* carries connotations of "polish" and "clean" as well as those of
a beautification process. I use "beauty treatment" here and at 2:12 (see
below) because it includes this sense while maintaining the over-
whelming emphasis of these passages on the women as objects of beauty.
That is, the process here is to prepare young women who are "pleasing
to look at" for presentation to the king, that one might be "pleasing in
his eyes."

2 PALIMPSEST

1 The primary writings Derrida reads in this essay are the series of
"prefaces against the necessity of a preface" in Hegel's *Phenomenology
of Spirit* (1807). Ironically, these prefaces focus largely on issues of
identity and subjectivity. For a full exegetical discussion, see especially
Nancy's "Identity and Trembling" (in 1993: 9–35).

2 On reading Esther in terms of plot reversal patterns, see especially Fox
(1983: 291–304; 1991b: 158–63), who presents a very convincing reading
of the book of Esther in terms of Aristotelian *peripety*, according to
which the result of an action turns out to be the exact reverse of what
was expected (e.g., Est 9:1). See also Sandra Beth Berg (1979: 103–13;
1980: 115–18), who largely follows Fox (referring to a pre-publication
copy of his 1983 essay). The discussion is expanded in terms of multiple
ironies by Stan Goldman (1990: 15–31).

3 Note also how the word order here (beginning with "a Jewish man" or
"Judean man" [see below]) also emphasizes the issue of Jewish identity.

4 This verse, of course, also links Mordecai's beginnings with those of
Daniel. See, e.g., Fewell (1992: 11–20) and Humphreys (1973).

5 I use the term "fostering" for *'omen* here because it implies Mordecai's

legal role as foster parent to his cousin as well as a more generic sense of "rearing" or "upbringing."

6 It is widely agreed, following the Targums, that the name Hadassah is Hebrew meaning "myrtle" (cf. Isaiah 41:19; 55:13; Zechariah 1:8, 10, 11). Most see this as the Hebrew name, and Esther as the Persian one (cf. Daniel 1:7), related to either Ishtar or Persian *stâra*, "star" (see Moore 1971: 20–1). Be that as it may, the irony that her so-imagined non-Jewish name, when inscribed in Hebrew, can also mean "I will hide" will remain significant for my reading. See especially my Conclusion.

7 This clearly refers to Esther's figure (see Haupt 1907–8; and cf. Genesis 29:17; 1 Samuel 25:3).

8 Baudrillard (1990: esp. 6–8) describes seduction (*se ducere*, "to lead away") as a strategy of appearances acted out by an object, which may have subversive implications for identity politics, especially with regard to sex. The object of the gaze, playing on surface appearances, leads the trusting, gazing subject away, beyond fixed oppositions such as masculine/feminine, subject/object, possession/lack, etc.

9 This statement from Butler, like many others in *Gender Trouble*, is explicitly an interpretation of Beauvoir's famous statement, "One is not born, but rather becomes, a woman" (1989: 267). See my discussion of Butler in Chapter 7.

10 Throughout these interchanges, Esther is the only woman who is literally "taken" (the verb used is *laqah*). This happens three times as she is taken by Mordecai into his house (i.e., "as daughter") and then to the king's house. The object slot for this verb is reserved for her, and this serves within the rhetoric of the narrative to reinforce a sense of her ostensibly passive object status. Whereas the young women generally are subjects of the verb "to go" (*bo'*; 2:13, 14), Esther is taken, first as a daughter (2:7, 15) and then into the king's house (2:16). On the taking of women in the books of Samuel, see Linafelt (1992).

11 Note that the date mentioned in 2:16 indicates that it has been about four years since he threw his first drinking party, which was "in the third year of his reign" (2:3).

12 The word for "gift" (*mas'et*) is related to the verb used to describe Esther's gaining (*nasa'*) of favor and support, thus suggesting a kind of reciprocation in the king's actions here. The qualifying phrase "as the king could afford" is somewhat odd. At the very least it indicates that gifts of differing amounts were given to different recipients based on their relation to the king (like dividends).

3 THE BIBLE AS MORAL LITERATURE

1 For more on the Bible, the politics of identity and the Christian right, see Beal and Gunn (1997: esp. xii–xiii, 1–12, 85–112, and 242–61).

2 For example, based on the fact that seven eunuchs were summoned to bring Vashti into the king's presence, she writes that seven separate *messages* were sent, one by each eunuch. After Vashti's refusal, moreover, she has the people attending the party go away immediately, "silent

NOTES

and ashamed." The counsel about what should be done to Vashti (when Memucan makes his recommendation) then takes place the next day. She also adds "of rare intelligence" to the biblical description of Esther in 2:7, which only mentions her appealing looks.

3 See also André LaCocque (1990: 49–83). His focus on Judith, Susanna, Esther, and Ruth as Jewish Second-Commonwealth literature of protest against patriarchal gender roles established in other biblical texts has great potential for exploring the relations between gender and ethnicity in identity politics. In the end, however, this study, too, remains bound to the basic issues and questions of "images of women" criticism. He intentionally distances himself, for example, from questions of Jewish identity in order to sharpen his focus on evaluation of the character of Esther. Even still, he sees this as a difficult task: "Were our topic the so-called Jewish question . . . no other document of the Bible would provide more arresting terms and more provocative perspectives. Our problem is the character of Esther . . ." (1990: 49). His evaluation of Esther is, like Fox's (1981b) and White's (1989), very positive (e.g., 1990: 51). Although the strong claim of the book is that these model heroines problematize traditional bipolar gender construction, in fact, for LaCocque, they appear to correct it and make it, once again, properly relational (heterosexual) and complementary. Their true "femininity," it would appear, emerges especially in their "style" of "*substitutional self-offering*" (118). This identity is secured and guaranteed especially by their linkage to God's plan of salvation history. Thus the religious dimensions so important for discussions of canonicity become primary here as well. Indeed, he makes clear their *essential* role in the forward march of salvation history, in a way similar to Anderson (1950) with regard to the Jews: "Keeping their memory alive thus becomes a prayer that there will always be servants to the Lord ready synergetically to make real God's kingship over history" (1990: 118).

4 In another article (1985: 137), Fuchs also identifies Esther with other female biblical characters who have been framed as "deceptive" in service of what is, in her view, the irredeemable patriarchal gynophobia that pervades all biblical literature. On the other hand, based on analysis of several biblical texts including Esther from the perspective of folklore studies, Susan Niditch (1987: xi) has suggested that "throughout its history, Israel has had a peculiar self-image as the underdog and the trickster." If this is so, and I agree with Niditch that it is, then the androcentric viewpoint of biblical discourse is, in this moment of subjective ambivalence, identifying with such women rather than simply repelling them phobically. See also Claudia V. Camp (1985: esp. 143–7).

5 Alice Laffey (1988: 216), like Paton (1908a: 96), also claims that Esther *uses* Vashti's misfortune to her own gain. Yet, as both White (1989: 176) and Fox (1991b: 207) point out, Esther did not seek to enter the harem after Vashti's banishment, but was brought there. This does not mean, however, that the book is not using Vashti's refusal and subsequent banishment as a way to get Esther up the Persian social ladder (see Niditch 1987: 133–4).

6 Although Fox's comment here is extremely insightful, his "excursus" is

130

not well integrated into the rest of his excellent exegetical and ideological-critical text work. It appears as a sort of mid-book appendix. Thus the two issues of identity remain isolated from one another within the book. One reason for this may be the form of the book, which is very much that of a commentary (probably the finest available) and topic-oriented critical introduction. Fox's primary engagement of Fuchs and Laffey in the "excursus," moreover, holds his focus on the issues demarcated by the "images of women" approach, and precludes a more in-depth analysis of how gender gets coded and negotiated in the first place. His awareness of the problematics of such dynamics in Esther is nonetheless clear. Moreover, his study of character in Esther, as it is related to the author's particular ideology (understood as his political interest in presenting the story as he does), provides many important insights, especially in its emphasis on the historical context of diaspora Judaism in Persia. Although often moving in very different directions, my study here is indebted to his two books (1991a; 1991b) at many key points.

7 Indeed, the greatest force of early deconstructions by Jacques Derrida on Hegel and Plato (e.g., 1981: 1–59, 61–171) and by Luce Irigaray on Freud (1985a: 11–129) is clearly exegetical. See also Beal (1997: 2–3).

4 WRITING OUT, II

1 On *sap* as literal "threshold" between two spaces, cf. Judges 19:27; 1 Kings 14:7; Isaiah 6:4; and Amos 9:1. The word is also often used in conjunction with the verb "to keep" or "guard" (e.g., Jeremiah 35:4; 52:24; 2 Kings 12:10?; 22:4?; 2 Chronicles 23:4; 25:18; 34:9; and Esther 9:2, on which see below). I use "keepers" rather than "guards" in order to maintain a closer parallel to its use to describe the two other eunuchs (Heggai and Shaashgaz) as "keepers of the women/concubines" previously.

2 There is a long-standing argument about whether *sarîs* in the Hebrew Bible refers to actual eunuch-hood (related to cognate verbs meaning "to castrate") or simply to a kind of "officer." In 2 Kings 22:9, for example, the term refers to an errand-runner. In Genesis 37–8 it appears to refer to a high foreign official. While the older argument that Nehemiah (cf. Nehemiah 1:11) was an actual eunuch has clearly lost ground over the past half-century (see North 1992: 87; and Yamauchi 1980: 132–42), this is not the case with regard to biblical references to foreign eunuchs. Indeed, as Paton (1908a: 148) rightly points out, the fact that the eunuchs in Esther often are the ones having access to women's quarters would suggest that they are, in fact, castrated personnel (cf., e.g., Herodotus viii.105).

3 The theme of conspiring eunuchs is a commonplace in world literature. It may also be evident in other biblical literature, particularly in the story of Jezebel's demise in 2 Kings 9. Jehu calls up to the window, "'Who is on my side? Who?' Two or three eunuchs looked out at him. He said, 'Throw her down.' So they threw her down . . ." (2 Kings 9:32–3).

4 Note how this tension is exploited further in the two Greek versions of

Esther (AT and LXX), where Haman first appears in an earlier plot against the king, which Mordecai had disclosed (Addition A). See Beal (1995).

5 On this intertextual relation, see especially McKane (1961: 260–1) and Magonet (1980).

6 The first four radicals in the Hitpael form of the verb "do obeisance" as it occurs here (*m-sh-t-h* with a hard het, ח), along with the phrase "for thus the king had commanded," provide an intriguing textual play on the earlier "drinking fest" (*m-sh-t-h* with a soft hey, ה) in chapter 1, which the king had also commanded (1:8), and which climaxed with Vashti's refusal. This deepens the relation between these two episodes and further identifies Mordecai as other with Vashti as other.

7 This set of identifications may be encouraged further by mention of Haman's "seat" or "throne" in 3:1 (cf. the king's "throne" in 1:2). This identification continues through 3:15. See below.

8 Significantly, this same phrase was used in 1:17 by Memucan in anticipation of the contempt women would show their men upon hearing of Vashti, which would result in "plenty of contempt."

9 It is noted further that both Haman's speech here and Memucan's previously introduce the proposed action with "If it pleases the king" (*'im 'al hammelek tôb*; 1:19 and 3:9).

10 The request to "let it be written" (*yiktab*) was also made by Memucan (1:19), thus further linking the two proposals.

11 *nabôkah* ("was in turmoil") is a Niphal form of *b-w-k*, a fairly uncommon verb meaning "to stir up" or "confuse." It carries the connotation of chaos or wandering in confusion. It is used, for example, to describe the Israelites under attack by Pharoah in Exodus 14:3. See also Joel 1:18; and Jastrow (1982: 145) on its use in Genesis Rabbah at the beginning of section 87.

5 FINDING ONESELF SIGNED UP

1 For a rather personal account of Lacan's hubris, his control of others more insecure than he, and his almost evangelical interests in establishing a totalizing movement of thought, see François Roustang (1990: 3–17).

2 Levinas's description of the fecundity of the caress, for example, "consists, therefore, not in approaching the other in its most vital dimension, the touch, but in the reduction of that vital dimension of the other's body to the elaboration of a future for himself" (Irigaray 1991: 110).

3 Turning Levinas's language about the caress slightly, Irigaray writes of this as the moment of fecundity without arrival, or birth, of the subject. "In that place, nothing attests to the subject" (Irigaray 1986: 238).

4 E.g., Levinas's discussion of creation and sexual difference in *Nine Talmudic Readings* (1990: 161–77), although this is an analysis of the Talmudic readings of Genesis (esp. 2:7), and not necessarily an espousal of them.

5 Quoting Freud: "Woman is a woman as a result of a certain lack of characteristics" (Irigaray 1985a: 112).

6 Within Lacan's psychosexual development schema, the boy's resolution of the Oedipal crisis is the definitive movement of that subject into the realm of the symbolic order, or Law of the Father, which introduces a triadic (linguistic) system of difference over against the imaginary's dualistic identification, and which represents, for Lacan, mature psychic identity. The Oedipal crisis involves the introduction of the father, a third party, into the diadic relation of mother and child. The imagined rivalry between child and father over the mother leads to the prohibition of access to the mother and her body. This is the first signification of the Law of the Father: prohibition, loss, separation. Thus the boy's psychological, and sexual-political, task is to abandon the mother and identify with the Law of the Father. For the girl in the castration complex, the movement is related: her task is to accept her lack (of a penis), and her place as woman in the order of things, turning her desire away from the mother (who has no penis) and toward the father. Thus the (overwhelmingly patriarchal and heterosexist) symbolic order becomes operational within the family economy (*oikonomia*, "house law"). For a full discussion of Lacan's model, see especially Kaja Silverman (1983: 149–93).

7 Within this theoretical model, Lacan uses the term "Other" (*Autre* with capital *A*) primarily in reference to the Law of the Father, the signification of lack (and therefore desire), or the Phallus, for both men and women. Located endosomatically with the unconscious, this Other is the governor and guarantor of the symbolic order, and therefore of male and female identity. The Other, then, is understood both as the foundation for the construction of the subject and as the structure that produces that subject. See below on the "Phallus" in Lacan. This use of the term is different from the uses one finds in most feminist theory, which follows Beauvoir.

8 Cf. Lacan (1981: 203), and the following passage from "The Function and Field of Speech and Language":

> Symbols in fact envelop the life of man in a network so total that they join together, before he comes into the world, those who are going to engender him "by flesh and blood"; so total that they bring to his birth, along with the gifts of the stars, if not with the gifts of the fairies, the shape of his destiny.
>
> (in 1977: 68)

9 See especially Lacan's "The Signification of the Phallus" (in 1977: 281–91). For a fuller discussion of the debate on Lacan and phallocentrism in feminist theory, see especially Gallop (1985: 133–56; 1982).

10 Just as it is wrong to identify Irigaray with Levinas altogether, it is likewise a mistake to conflate the writings of Beauvoir and Irigaray, for there are highly significant differences between them. Irigaray has recently noted (1993: 9–11) that one major difference is her training in and commitment to psychoanalysis for theorizing sexual difference. Ironically, the aspect of Freudian psychoanalysis that Irigaray has the most occasion to criticize, namely the view that the sexual development of girls and boys unfolds in the same way, is often assumed by Beauvoir

(see, e.g., Irigaray 1985a: 25–6; and 1985b: 34–5; and cf. Beauvoir 1989: 267–8). Indeed, as already noted, questioning this assumption, wherever it emerges, is central in Irigaray's analysis of the phallocratic "Logic of the Same," by which alterity is reduced and objectified. Another difference between the two writers, on my reading, is Irigaray's less dismissive treatment of various forms of women's subjectivity within phallocracy that Beauvoir condemned as delusional (e.g., the mystic's effort to "transform her prison into a heaven of glory, her servitude into sovereign liberty" [Beauvoir 1989: 628]; cf., on the other hand, Irigaray on *La Mystérique* [1985a: 191–202]).

11 It should be noted that Irigaray's book *Speculum of the Other Woman* is "organized" gynecologically. That is, it is shaped like a hollow, or concave, space of multiple surfaces (counter-phallic). The two outside folds are close readings of Freud and Plato. The center section is titled "Speculum." About the book's shape, Irigaray herself comments (1985b: 68), "*Speculum* has no beginning or end. The architectonics of the text, or texts, confounds the linearity of an outline, the teleology of discourse, within which there is no possible place for the 'feminine,' except the traditional place of the repressed, the censured. Furthermore, by 'beginning' with Freud and 'ending' with Plato we are already going at history 'backwards.' But it is a reversal 'within' which the question of the woman still cannot be articulated, so this reversal alone does not suffice. That is why, in the book's 'middle' texts – *Speculum*, once again – the reversal seemingly disappears."

12 In Derridean language, one might put it that difference for Irigaray always implies *différance*: rather than bouncing straight back to a binary oppositional subject, there is deferral, a kind of semiotic slippage that resists structural closure and stability.

13 The sense of this Hitpalpal form (appearing only here) of *ḥûl* is that of writhing in anxiety or agitation. While it does connote suffering, it does *not* necessarily carry any sense of lament or mourning, which would put her in solidarity with the other Jews who are mourning.

6 INSOMNIA AND A LOST DREAM OF WRITING

1 The text does not indicate whether she touched the scepter with her hand or her lips, and in fact many artistic renderings depict her kneeling before him with her lips on the scepter.

2 The verb used here, often translated as "to turn toward," is actually a verbal form of "face," thus this is literally a face-to-face encounter. The same word is at the root of the phrase "in the presence of" (*lipnê*; lit. "to the face of"), which was discussed earlier.

3 Interestingly, the verb "to seek" (*baqash*) has been used previously in Esther with reference to seeking harm: the eunuchs "sought to lay hands on the king" (2:21); and Haman "sought to wipe out all the Jews" (3:6). Here, then, there may be the trace of an allusion to what Esther seeks ultimately (i.e., the demise of an enemy).

4 The text more literally reads, "and upon looking at [$w^ekir'ôt$ ... 'et] Mordecai." This establishes a further link between this episode and the conflict in chapter 1, as well as further identification between Mordecai and Vashti, for a very similar infinitive construct described the men looking at her as well (with a lamed preposition ["*to* look at"] rather than a kaph ["*upon*" or "*while* looking at"]).

5 The verb translated as "tremble" (z-w-') is uncommon in biblical Hebrew, but usually signifies physical shaking (of a person or of the earth; cf. Jastrow 1982: 388–9). I take it here to suggest that Mordecai did not behave with reverence before Haman and yet showed no fear for his own welfare.

6 This verse involves an odd combination of earlier actions by the king with regard to Vashti's refusal, for the king had summoned Vashti to come (as Haman now summons his friends and wife), and had sought advice from those near him (as Haman seeks from the people he summons to be near him).

7 SUBVERSIVE EXCESSES

1 Foucault's focus in *History of Sexuality* is the specific issue of modern sexuality in the West, arguing, against mechanistic understandings of repression, that sexuality is a production of power rather than a repression of desire (e.g., 1978: 114; cf. 1984: 62).

2 There are, of course, important differences between Butler and Irigaray on issues of sexual identity and sexual difference. Compare, for example, the introductions to Butler's *Bodies that Matter* (1993: 1–16) and Irigaray's recent *Je, Tu, Nous* (1993: 9–14). For Butler's reading of Irigaray's reading of Plato in *Speculum*, see Butler (1993: 36–49).

3 Irigaray's strategy of *mimesis* is another example of what Butler calls subversive confusion. By *mimesis* feminine and masculine subject positions are thwarted by unpredictable or out-of-place repetitions. See, e.g., Irigaray (1985b: 76); see also her mimetic first-person appropriation of Freud's lecture style in the beginning of *Speculum*, and her subsequent series of quotations without comment from Plotinus (1985a: 168–79). A recent example of this practice is The Breeders' cover version of Aerosmith's misogynous song, "Lord of the Thighs" (Electra, 1993).

4 On Lacan and the biblical God, see especially the Bible and Culture Collective (1995: 201–10).

8 COMING OUT

1 The end of this speech (verse 4b), which is not included in the quotation here, is difficult to translate. I agree with Haupt (1907–8: 146) that the basic sense is that it would not be worthwhile to annoy the king on account of the enemy if it were not for the extremity of the situation. Thus, my translation is, "If only we were sold as servants and as maids, I would keep silent, for [then] the adversary would not be worth the king's trouble."

2 See also the king's subsequent denouncement of Haman in 9:25: "Let the evil plot, which *he* devised against the Jews, recoil on *his own* head!" In fact, as was evident in 3:15, the king himself and his law were quite completely aligned with Haman over against the Jews.

3 The sense of *ba'at* is that of being startled or disturbed to the point of terror. Interestingly, the word occurs primarily in Job, and usually describes Job's oppression by God (e.g., 3:5; 7:14; 9:34; 13:11, 21; 15:24; 18:11; and 33:7). Cf. Daniel 8:17, and especially 1 Samuel 16:15, where it refers to the terror experienced by Saul after God sends an evil spirit on him, dooming him and his reign. Significantly, this follows immediately after the passage in 1 Samuel 15, discussed earlier, in which the Benjamite Saul is criticized for keeping booty after defeating Agag.

4 Haman's infamy and doom are accentuated by the comment that "as the words left the mouth of the king, they covered Haman's face." This parallels the terror invoked by Esther's words in 7:6. The image of covering the face is used in 6:12 as well to describe the humiliation Haman experienced from bestowing the king's honor on Mordecai.

5 Magonet (1980) rightly comments that the overcoming of Haman the Agagite by Mordecai the Benjamite is a *tikkun*, or healing, of Saul's failure against Agag in 1 Samuel 15 (see my earlier discussions of Magonet). Chapter 9 also represents a *tikkun* of the people's failure not to take booty in that earlier story, for it insistently asserts that in their fighting they "took no booty" (9:10, 15, 16). Of course, as my analysis of the book of Esther makes clear, Mordecai's overcoming of Haman is not nearly all his own doing. Indeed, in both cases (1 Samuel 15 and Esther), there is a strong sense of inadvertency and accident in both outcomes, which has testified for many commentators to the secret, hidden workings of God in the stories (see esp. Cohen 1974; and see my discussion of hiding in the next chapter).

6 Koehler-Baumgartner has *"sich als Juden bezeichnen"* (roughly, "declared themselves as Jews"). Along similar lines, the LXX and Old Latin both include that they were circumcised. The AT has many Jews circumcising themselves without opposition from other people. Perhaps the closest textual comparison would be with the Greek apocryphal addition to Daniel, *Bel and the Dragon*, where the Persian people express frustration that their king has "become a Jew" (*Ioudaios gegonen ho Basileus*; v. 28). There are significant points of contrast as well, however. First, this Greek text has no verb equivalent to "to jew," thus diminishing the sense of Jewish identity as performative, a matter of on-going behavior/appearance. Second, *Bel and the Dragon* is pervaded by divine presence and Daniel's devotion to Jewish worship practices, so that the sense of the king's "becoming a Jew" is that of religious conversion. In Esther, however, there has been little if anything religious to attribute to Jewish identity.

See also the Greek word *ioudaizein*, literally "to jew," in Galatians 2:14. Interestingly, this is the only verbal form of "Jew" (*ioudaios*) in the New Testament. The issue in Galatians is whether or not gentiles need to become Jews in order to become Christians. Paul is arguing against those who teach that the Galatians must be Jewish, that is, keep

Torah (including circumcision). Luther's use, discussed in my introduction, of "Judaizing" as a negative term which he opposes to living under grace by faith – according to spirit rather than flesh – is closely related to Galatians. I am thankful to Gary Phillips for drawing my attention to this passage.

7 Compare the phrase used here to describe the Jewish defense ("to stand up for their lives") with that describing Haman's action in 7:7 ("he stood to seek his life").

8 I am following the Tanakh translation here ("together with women and children"). Gordis (1976: 49–53), followed by Magonet (1980: 168), has argued that this verse does not indicate that the Jews were to massacre women and children. Rather, he claims, the reference should be understood here as an included quotation. That is, the Jews are to slaughter any people or province attacking the Jew(ish males), their Jewish women and their Jewish children, as decreed in Est 3:13. This is not likely, however, given that this decree otherwise calls for a total reversal of the former one. The sense here is that of complete turnabout.

9 As already noted, the Jews do *not* take booty, even though the king permits it. And indeed, the only mention of the Jews slaughtering women or children, even though the king permits it, is found in their killing and hanging of Haman's ten sons (9:12, 14).

10 One exception, as Fox notes (1991b: 223 n. 16), is Paul Haupt (1906), who, as he was analyzing this part of the text of Esther, was receiving news of the slaughter of thousands of Jews in Odessa. Perhaps the telegraphs describing those barbarisms served as a sort of encoded face-to-face encounter for him with the other Jew, deciphered onto the book of Esther, which made it impossible for him to read the book as it had so often been read before.

IN CONCLUSION

1 That Sedgwick uses Racine's spellings of the names in the story indicates that his is the primary text, which she approaches via Proust. Thus the biblical narrative, which is my focus, is twice removed in Sedgwick's analogy.

2 Fox is right to interpret the book of Esther on the whole as being "comfortable with the idea of the Jews living among the nations indefinitely ... accepted for the most part as equals" (1991b: 219 *et passim*). There is no indication in the book that Jews in Persian diaspora would or should have wanted to distinguish themselves over against Persian society (only Haman claims that they did so), or to "return" to Palestine. This is a story about Jews in diaspora for the long haul. It is a mistake, however, to assume further that Jewish identification was perceived in Esther as carrying no risk whatsoever. Although it cannot be assumed that in Esther Jewishness implies marginal status, it is equally mistaken to imagine that there was no risk, even before Haman's decree, in the identification. Esther is concerned with identity politics in the Jewish diaspora and with the phenomenon of anti-Judaism, not simply

NOTES

with the particular anti-Judaism of some anomalous historical figure
named Haman. Certainly the fact that the law calling for the annihilation
of all Jews, which the king in fact wholly endorses, incites such a fury
of public preparations for "that day" would suggest that there was
something there already, waiting for a spark to ignite it into flames. The
power of this book rests largely on one's sense that the risks involved in
its play are very, very real.
3 See, e.g., Foucault (1978), Bray (1982), and Katz (1983).
4 Signs of this ambivalence continue to be prevalent. Consider contemporary American Protestantism, in which questions of gay/straight
identity have figured prominently over the last decade or so. In its 1996
meeting, for example, the General Assembly of the Presbyterian Church
(USA) – my own church affiliation – approved homophobic legislation
that would allow people who are homosexual to be ordained *only so long
as they remain celibate*, implying a split between homosexual activity
and homosexual identity. The genital act is prohibited, but the self-
definition is not. The message: *be* one, but don't *do* one. Many believe
that this decision will lead to "witch hunts" (another trope, with yet
another historical context, which often plays a part in contemporary
discourse about homosexuality in the church), looking for actions to
match the definition. On the other hand, if one watches Christian cable
television or listens to Christian talk radio as much as I do, one can see
that among conservative evangelical and fundamentalist Christians,
homosexuality is not a matter of self-evident identity, but of sexual
activity: one can *become* straight by abstaining from homosexual
activity. A term often used in this context is *metanoia*, which means both
to repent and to turn around 180 degrees.
5 This ambiguity is both physical (as castrates) and social (without family,
occupying women's quarters, mediating between the sexes).
6 Note also Haman's convergence with Memucan (1:16–20; 3:1–15), which
is related to his identification with the king (3:8–15; 5:9–14; 6:7–9). Just
as Vashti leaves traces on Mordecai and Esther, so Memucan leaves traces
on Haman, another royal advisor who, through political discourse with
the king, marks the other for oblivion and thereby shores up his identity
with the king over against that other. So common are their identities that
Targum Rishon introduces Memucan as "Memukhan, who is Haman,
grandson of Agag the evil one" (1:16; see also Megilla 12b and Midrash
Esther Rabba). For the reader, of course, this further supports identification with Vashti and Mordecai over against him. That is, if there was
any doubt about Memucan being "evil," as the Targum puts it, the
identification of him with Haman (and, relatedly, of Vashti with
Mordecai) clears it away. Still, Haman and Memucan diverge in their
ends. Memucan finishes his part in the story by pleasing the king (1:21);
Haman, by contrast, finds himself terror-stricken in the presence of both
Esther and a very displeased king (7:6–8). Haman's end is a shameful
death. Whereas a word went out from the presence of the king to write
off Vashti's offense at the end of chapter 1, in 7:8 "the word went
out of the king's mouth" and covered "Haman's face." Thus in the
game of pleasing the king in his presence, Memucan defeats Vashti, while

138

Esther and Mordecai defeat Haman. Esther reconfigures and redeploys *Haman's* identity convergences when she redeploys her own, insofar as her action leads to Haman's dis-identification from the king and his full identification (at the stake) with Bigthan and Teresh (7:9–10). See Beal (1995: 107–10).

7 Note also his ultimate identification with the insurrectory eunuchs, political enemies of the king, at the stake. The Greek versions (LXX and AT) of Esther sharpen this identification by introducing him as their compatriot (Addition A). See Beal (1995: 107–10).

8 The final thesis of this analysis, which is not quoted here, was added shortly after the war (Adorno and Horkheimer 1991: xvii).

9 The unpointed Hebrew text is nearly identical to Esther's name, which can be parsed as a first-person perfect form of the Hebrew verb *satar.* See also Genesis 4:14, in which Cain is told that God will hide [אסתר] from his face. Notice that in that passage, which is similar to Deuteronomy 31:18, the unpointed Hebrew text is exactly the same as Esther's name. Cf. Talmud Megillah 13a, in which R. Judah says that, although Hadassah was her original, she was called Esther because she "hid facts about herself."

10 It is important to note that this argument can only be a *canonical* one. The book's canonical context should not be confused with other ancient cultural contexts. One cannot argue, for example, that the book's lack of explicit references to religion or the deity would have made it unique as a Jewish text at a given time and place within diaspora Judaism during the Second Temple period. It could just as well be that the book is the only remaining fragment of a vast corpus of such ostensibly non-religious texts concerned with Jewish identity and its ambiguities.

11 I.e., fasting (4:16), lamenting in sackcloth and ashes (4:1–4), and not touching the plunder (9:10, 15, 16). None of these, moreover, need be construed as exclusively Jewish religious practices.

12 For Jewish mysticism, the greater the treasure, the greater the blockades to reaching it. The *pardes*, or mystical garden, in which the "there is" (*yesh*) might be encountered, is heavily gated. For this tradition, especially in the late twelfth- or early thirteenth-century additions to the *Zohar* (see *Ra'ya Mehemna* and *Tikkunei Zohar*), the obvious obstacles to a theological reading of Esther become portals onto a mystical book of hiding. In them both Esther and the king are often manifestations of the divine. Esther is adorned as *Shekinah*, divine presence, coupled with the k/King in the palace garden/Garden of Eden, signifying the end of exile.

13 On Job as a faultline in "the biblical," see also Linafelt (1996: 1–18) and Beal (1996, forthcoming).

14 See especially Fewell and Gunn (1993: 94–186); Newsom (1989: 142–60); and Camp (1997: 85–112).

15 In this sense deconstruction is by no means apolitical or even a deconstruction of politics, as some have argued; on the contrary, it opens new possibilities of political transformation by showing that the very categories of identity themselves are political. Cf. Sedgwick (1990: 83) and Butler (1990: 148).

NOTES

16 Kenneth Craig (1995: 157–65; cf. Gaster 1950) has shown that Purim's carnivalesque character may go all the way back to, and in fact be rooted in, the earliest developments of the literary history of the Esther tale. However, as he and others point out (e.g., Jacobs 1971), the emphasis on masquerading ("mummeries") appears to have gained dominance much later, perhaps in the sixteenth century. Nonetheless, based on my analysis of the text of Esther, I am arguing that such masquerading practices are particularly appropriate.

BIBLIOGRAPHY

Adorno, Theodor and Max Horkheimer (1991) *Dialectic of Enlightenment*, trans. John Cumming, New York: Continuum.
Anderson, Bernhard W. (1950) "The Place of the Book of Esther in the Christian Bible," *Journal of Religion* 30: 32–43.
—— (1986) *Understanding the Old Testament*, fourth edn, Englewood Cliffs, NJ: Prentice-Hall.
Anderson, Bernhard W. and Arthur C. Lichtenberger (1954) "The Book of Esther," *Interpreter's Dictionary of the Bible* III: 821–74.
Bal, Miecke (1992) "Lots of Writing," *Semeia* 54: 77–99.
Bardtke, Hans (1964) "Luther und das Buch Esther," *Sammlung gemeinverständlicher Vorträge und Schriften aus dem Gebiet der Theologie und Religionsgeschichte* 240,41: 81–5.
—— (1965–6) "Neuere Arbeiten zum Esterbuch: Ein kritische Würdigung," *Ex Oriente Lux* 19: 519–49.
Bataille, Georges (1989) *Theory of Religion*, trans. Robert Hurley, New York: Zone Books.
Baudrillard, Jean (1990) *Seduction*, New York: St. Martin's Press.
Beal, Timothy K. (1992) "Ideology and Intertextuality: Surplus of Meaning and Controlling the Means of Production," in Danna Nolan Fewell (ed.) *Reading Between Texts: Intertextuality and the Hebrew Bible*, Louisville: Westminster/John Knox.
—— (1994) "The System and the Speaking Subject in the Hebrew Bible: Reading for Divine Abjection," *Biblical Interpretation* 2: 171–89.
—— (1995) "Tracing Esther's Beginnings," in Athalya Brenner (ed.) *A Feminist Companion to Esther, Judith, and Susanna*, Sheffield: Sheffield Academic Press.
—— (1996, forthcoming) "Facing Job," *Semeia: Levinas and the Bible*.
—— (1997) "Opening: Cracking the Binding," in Timothy K. Beal and David M. Gunn (eds) *Reading Bibles, Writing Bodies: Identity and The Book*, London and New York: Routledge.
Beal, Timothy K. and David M. Gunn (eds) (1997) *Reading Bibles, Writing Bodies: Identity and The Book*, London and New York: Routledge.
Beauvoir, Simone de (1989) *The Second Sex*, trans. H. M. Parshley, New York: Vintage.

141

Berg, Sandra Beth (1979) *The Book of Esther: Motifs, Themes, and Structure*, Missoula: Scholars Press.

—— (1980) "After the Exile: God and History in the Books of the Chronicles and Esther," in J. L. Crenshaw and S. Sandmel (eds) *The Divine Helmsman*, New York: Ktav.

Bhabha, Homi K. (1994) *The Location of Culture*, London and New York: Routledge.

Bible and Culture Collective (1995) *The Postmodern Bible*, New Haven and London: Yale University Press.

Bickerman, Elias J. (1967) *Four Strange Books of the Bible: Jonah, Daniel, Koheleth, Esther*, New York: Schocken.

—— (1988) *The Jews in the Greek Age*, Cambridge, MA and London: Harvard University Press.

Boyarin, Daniel (1994) *A Radical Jew: Paul and the Politics of Identity*, Berkeley: University of California Press.

—— (1997) "'An Imaginary and Desirable Converse': *Moses and Monotheism* as Family Romance," in Timothy K. Beal and David M. Gunn (eds) *Reading Bibles, Writing Bodies: Identity and The Book*, London and New York: Routledge.

Boyarin, Jonathan (1992) *Storm from Paradise: The Politics of Jewish Memory*, Minneapolis: University of Minnesota Press.

Bray, Alan (1982) *Homosexuality in Renaissance England*, London: Gay Men's Press.

Brenner, Athalya (ed.) (1995) *A Feminist Companion to Esther, Judith, and Susanna*, Sheffield: Sheffield Academic Press.

Brown, Jerald M. (1976) "Rabbinic Interpretations of the Characters and Plot of the Book of Esther," Rabbinical thesis, Hebrew Union College/Jewish Institute of Religion.

Butler, Judith (1990) *Gender Trouble: Feminism and the Subversion of Identity*, New York and London: Routledge.

—— (1993) *Bodies that Matter: On the Discursive Limits of "Sex,"* New York and London: Routledge.

Camp, Claudia V. (1985) *Wisdom and the Feminine in the Book of Proverbs*, Sheffield: Almond Press.

—— (1997) "Woman Wisdom and the Strange Woman: Where is Power to be Found?," in Timothy K. Beal and David M. Gunn (eds) *Reading Bibles, Writing Bodies: Identity and The Book*, London and New York: Routledge.

Cazelles, Henri (1961) "Note sur la composition du rouleau d'Esther," in H. Gross and F. Mussner (eds) *Lex tua veritas: Festschrift für Hubert Junker*, Trier: Paulinus.

Cixous, Hélène (1976) "The Laugh of the Medusa," *Signs* 1: 875–99.

—— (1991) "Coming to Writing," in Deborah Jenson (ed.) *"Coming to Writing" and Other Essays*, Cambridge, MA: Harvard University Press.

—— (1993a) "We Who Are Free, Are We Free?" *Critical Inquiry* 19: 201–19.

—— (1993b) "Without End no State of Drawingness no, rather: The Executioner's Taking off," *New Literary History* 24: 91–103.

BIBLIOGRAPHY

Clines, David J. A. (1984) *The Esther Scroll: The Story of the Story*, Sheffield: JSOT Press.

—— (1990) "Reading Esther from Left to Right: Contemporary Strategies for Reading a Biblical Text," in David J. A. Clines, Stephen E. Fowl, and Stanley E. Porter (eds) *The Bible in Three Dimensions*, Sheffield: JSOT Press.

—— (1991) "In Quest of the Historical Mordecai," *Vetus Testamentum* 41: 129–36.

Cohen, Abraham D. (1974) "'Hu Ha-goral': The Religious Significance of Esther," *Judaism* 23: 87–94.

Condamin, Albert (1898) "Notes critique sur la texte biblique, II. La disgrace d'Aman (Esth. VII.8)," *Revue biblique* 7: 253–61.

Cornell, Drucilla (1992) *Philosophy of the Limit*, New York and London: Routledge.

—— (1993) *Transformations: Recollective Imagination and Sexual Difference*, New York and London: Routledge.

Craig, Kenneth (1995) *Reading Esther: A Case for the Literary Carnivalesque*, Louisville: Westminster/John Knox.

Crenshaw, James L. (1976) "Method in Determining Wisdom Influence upon 'Historical' Literature," in James L. Crenshaw (ed.) *Studies in Ancient Israelite Wisdom*, New York: Ktav.

Davis, John (1977) *People of the Mediterranean: An Essay in Comparative Social Anthropology*, London: Routledge & Kegan Paul.

Derrida, Jacques (1981) *Dissemination*, trans. Barbara Johnson, Chicago: University of Chicago Press.

—— (1985) "The Original Discussion of '*Differance*' (1968)," in D. Wood and R. Bernasconi (eds) *Derrida and Differance*, Coventry: Parousia.

—— (1991) "Des Tours de Babel," *Semeia* 54: 3–34.

Detweiler, Robert (1991) "Overliving," *Semeia* 54: 239–55.

Dommershausen, Werner (1968) *Die Estherrolle: Stil und Ziel einer alttestamentlichen Schrift*, Stuttgart: Katholisches Bibelwerk.

Eckhardt, Roy (1974) *Your People, My People: The Meeting of Jews and Christians*, New York: Quadrangle.

Eilberg-Schwartz, Howard (1990) *The Savage in Judaism: An Anthropology of Israelite Religion and Ancient Judaism*, Bloomington: Indiana University Press.

Ewald, Heinrich G. A. (1869) *History of Israel, I*, English trans., London: Longmans, Green, and Company.

Fewell, Danna Nolan (1992) "Introduction: Writing, Reading, and Relating," in Danna Nolan Fewell (ed.) *Reading Between Texts: Intertextuality and the Hebrew Bible*, Louisville: Westminster/John Knox.

Fewell, Danna Nolan and David M. Gunn (1993) *Gender, Power, and Promise: The Subject of the Bible's First History*, Nashville: Abingdon.

Foucault, Michel (1977) "The Confession of the Flesh," in Colin Gordon (ed.) *Power/Knowledge: Selected Interviews and Other Writings 1972–1977*, New York: Pantheon.

—— (1978) *The History of Sexuality, Volume 1: An Introduction*, trans. Robert Hurley, New York: Vintage.

143

—— (1984) "Truth and Power," in Peter Rabinow (ed.) *The Foucault Reader*, New York: Pantheon.

Fox, Michael V. (1983) "The Structure of the Book of Esther," in A. Rofé and Y. Zakovitch (eds) *Isac Leo Seeligmann Memorial Volume*, Jerusalem.

—— (1991a) *The Redaction of the Book of Esther: On Reading Composite Texts*, Atlanta: Scholars Press.

—— (1991b) *Character and Ideology in the Book of Esther*, Columbia, SC: University of South Carolina Press.

Fuchs, Esther (1982) "Status and Role of Female Heroines in the Biblical Narrative," *Mankind Quarterly* 23: 149–60.

—— (1985) "Who Is Hiding the Truth? Deceptive Women and Biblical Androcentrism," in A. Y. Collins (ed.) *Feminist Perspectives on Biblical Scholarship*, Chico, CA: Scholars Press.

—— (1989) "The Literary Characterization of Mothers and Sexual Politics in the Hebrew Bible," *Semeia* 46: 151–66.

Gallop, Jane (1982) *The Daughters of Seduction: Feminism and Psychoanalysis*, Ithaca: Cornell University Press.

—— (1985) *Reading Lacan*, Ithaca: Cornell University Press.

Garber, Marjorie (1992) *Vested Interests: Cross-dressing & Cultural Anxiety*, New York and London: Routledge.

Gaster, Theodor H. (1950) *Purim and Hanukkah in Custom and Tradition*, New York: Henry Schuman.

Gerleman, Gilles (1966) "Studien zu Esther: Stoff–Struktur–Stil–Sinn," *Biblische Studien* 48: 1–48.

Gilman, Sander (1991) *The Jew's Body*, London and New York: Routledge.

Ginzberg, Louis (1941) *The Legends of the Jews, IV*, Philadelphia: Jewish Publication Society.

Goldman, Stan (1990) "Narrative and Ethical Ironies in Esther," *Journal for the Study of the Old Testament* 47: 15–31.

Gordis, Robert (1974) *Megillat Esther: The Masoretic Hebrew Text with Introduction, New Translation and Commentary*, New York: Ktav.

—— (1976) "Studies in the Esther Narrative," *Journal of Biblical Literature* 95: 43–58.

—— (1981) "Religion, Wisdom and History in the Book of Esther," *Journal of Biblical Literature* 100: 359–88.

Grossfeld, Bernard (1991) *The Two Targums of Esther, Translated, with Apparatus and Notes*, Aramaic Bible, 18. Collegeville, MN: Liturgical.

Handelman, Susan A. (1991) *Fragments of Redemption: Jewish Thought and Literary Theory in Benjamin, Scholem, and Levinas*, Bloomington: Indiana University Press.

Haupt, Paul (1906) "Purim," *Beiträge zur Assyriologie*: 1–28.

—— (1907–8) "Critical Notes on Esther," *American Journal of Semitic Languages and Literatures* 24: 97–186.

Horschander, Jacob (1923) *The Book of Esther in Light of History*, Philadelphia: Dropsie College.

Humphreys, W. Lee (1973) "A Life-style for Diaspora: A Study of the Tales of Esther and Daniel," *Journal of Biblical Literature* 92: 211–23.

Irigaray, Luce (1985a) *Speculum of the Other Woman*, trans. G. G. Gill, Ithaca: Cornell University Press.

—— (1985b) *This Sex Which Is Not One*, trans. Catherine Porter with Carolyn Burke, Ithaca: Cornell University Press.

—— (1986) "The Fecundity of the Caress," in R. A. Cohen (ed.) *Face to Face with Levinas*, Albany: SUNY Press.

—— (1991) "Questions to Emmanuel Levinas: On the Divinity of Love," in Robert Bernasconi and Simon Critchley (eds) *Re-Reading Levinas*, Bloomington: Indiana University Press.

—— (1993) *Je, Tu, Nous: Toward a Culture of Difference*, trans. A. Martin, New York and London: Routledge.

Jabès, Edmond (1993) *The Book of Margins*, trans. Rosemary Waldrop, Chicago: University of Chicago Press.

Jabès, Edmond with Emmanuel Levinas (1993) "There Is no Trace But in the Desert," in Edmond Jabès, *The Book of Margins*, trans. Rosemary Waldrop, Chicago: University of Chicago Press.

Jacobs, Louis (1971) "Purim," *Encyclopaedia Judaica* 13: 1390–95.

Jameson, Fredric (1981) *The Political Unconscious: Narrative as a Socially Symbolic Act*, Ithaca: Cornell University Press.

Jastrow, Marcus (1982) *A Dictionary of the Targumim: The Talmud Babli and Yerushalmi, and the Midrashic Literature*, New York: Judaica Press.

Katz, Jonathan (1983) *Gay/Lesbian Almanac: A New Documentary*, New York: Harper & Row.

Klein, Lillian R. (1995) "Honor and Shame in Esther," in Athalya Brenner (ed.) *A Feminist Companion to Esther, Judith, and Susanna*, Sheffield: Sheffield Academic Press.

Kristeva, Julia (1980) *Desire in Language: A Semiotic Approach to Literature and Art*, trans. T. Gora, A. Jardine, and L. Roudiez, New York: Columbia University Press.

—— (1982) *The Powers of Horror: An Essay on Abjection*, trans. L. Roudiez, New York: Columbia University Press.

—— (1984) *Revolution in Poetic Language*, trans. M. Waller, New York: Columbia University Press.

—— (1986) "The System and the Speaking Subject," in T. Moi (ed.) *The Kristeva Reader*, Chicago: University of Chicago Press.

Lacan, Jacques (1977) *Écrits: A Selection*, trans. Alan Sheridan, New York: Norton.

—— (1981) *The Four Fundamental Concepts of Psycho-Analysis*, trans. Alan Sheridan, New York: Norton.

LaCocque, André (1990) *The Feminine Unconventional: Four Subversive Figures in Israel's Tradition*, Philadelphia: Fortress Press.

Laffey, Alice (1988) *An Introduction to the Old Testament: A Feminist Perspective*, Philadelphia: Fortress Press.

Levinas, Emmanuel (1969) *Totality and Infinity: An Essay on Exteriority*, trans. Alphonso Lingis, Pittsburgh: Dusquesne University Press.

—— (1978) "Signature," *Research in Phenomenology* 8: 175–89.

—— (1981) *Otherwise than Being, or Beyond Essence*, trans. Alphonso Lingis, The Hague: Martinus Nijhoff.

—— (1985) *Ethics and Infinity: Conversations with Philippe Nemo*, trans. Richard A. Cohen, Pittsburgh: Duquesne University Press.

—— (1987) *Time and the Other*, trans. Richard A. Cohen, Pittsburgh: Duquesne University Press.

—— (1989a) "There is: Existence without Existents," in Seán Hand (ed.) *The Levinas Reader*, Cambridge, MA and Oxford: Blackwell.

—— (1989b) "God and Philosophy," in Seán Hand (ed.) *The Levinas Reader*, Cambridge, MA and Oxford: Blackwell.

—— (1990) *Nine Talmudic Readings by Emmanuel Levinas*, trans. Annette Aronowicz, Bloomington: Indiana University Press.

Linafelt, Tod (1992) "Taking Women in Samuel: Readers/Responses/Responsibility," in Danna Nolan Fewell (ed.) *Reading Between Texts: Intertextuality and the Hebrew Bible*, Louisville: Westminster/John Knox.

—— (1995) "Surviving Lamentations," *Horizons in Biblical Theology* 17: 45–61.

—— (1996) "The Undecidability of *barak* in the Prologue to Job," *Biblical Interpretation* 4: 1–18.

McKane, William (1961) "A Note on Esther IX and I Samuel XV," *Journal of Theological Studies* 12: 260–1.

Magonet, Jonathan (1980) "The Liberal and the Lady: Esther Revisited," *Judaism* 29: 167–76.

Meinhold, Arndt (1975) "Die Gattung des Josephsgeschichte und des Estherbuches: Diasporanovelle, I," *Zeitschrift für die alttestamentliche Wissenschaft* 87: 306–24.

—— (1976) "Die Gattung des Josephsgeschichte und des Estherbuches: Diasporanovelle, II," *Zeitschrift für die alttestamentliche Wissenschaft* 88: 72–93.

Moi, Toril (1985) *Sexual/Textual Politics: Feminist Literary Theory*, London and New York: Routledge.

Moore, Carey A. (1967) "A Greek Witness to a Different Hebrew Text of Esther," *Zeitschrift für die alttestamentliche Wissenschaft* 79: 351–8.

—— (1971) *Esther*, Garden City: Doubleday.

—— (1973) "On the Origins of the LXX Additions to the Book of Esther," *Journal of Biblical Literature* 92: 382–93.

—— (1977) *Daniel, Esther and Jeremiah: The Additions*, Garden City: Doubleday.

—— (ed.) (1982) *Studies in the Book of Esther*, New York: Ktav.

—— (1983) "Esther Revisited Again," *Hebrew Annual Review* 7: 169–85.

—— (1985) "Esther Revisited: An Examination of Esther Studies over the Past Decade," in A. Kort and S. Morschauser (eds) *Biblical Studies in Honor of Samuel Iwry*, Winona Lake: Eisenbrauns.

—— (1992) "Esther," *Anchor Bible Dictionary* 2: 633–43.

Nancy, Jean-Luc (1993) *The Birth to Presence*, trans. Brian Holmes *et al.*, Stanford: Stanford University Press.

Neusner, Jacob (1989) *Esther Rabba I: An Analytical Translation*, Brown Judaic Studies, 182. Atlanta: Scholars Press.

Newsom, Carol A. (1989) "Women and the Discourse of Patriarchal Wisdom: A Study of Proverbs 1–9," in P. L. Day (ed.) *Gender and Difference in Ancient Israel*, Minneapolis: Fortress Press. Revised and reprinted in Timothy K. Beal and David M. Gunn (eds) (1997) *Reading*

Bibles, Writing Bodies: Identity and The Book, London and New York: Routledge.

Newsom, Carol A. and Sharon H. Ringe (1992) *The Women's Bible Commentary*, Louisville: Westminster/John Knox.

Niditch, Susan (1987) *Underdogs and Tricksters*, San Francisco: Harper & Row.

North, Robert (1992) "Postexilic Judean Officials," *Anchor Bible Dictionary* 5: 86–90.

Olmstead, Albert T. (1948) *The History of the Persian Empire*, Chicago: University of Chicago Press.

Orlinsky, Harry M. (1974) "The Canonization of the Hebrew Bible and the Exclusion of the Apocrypha," in Harry M. Orlinsky (ed.) *Essays in Biblical and Jewish Culture and Bible Translation*, New York: Ktav.

Paton, Lewis Bayles (1908a) *The Book of Esther*, International Critical Commentary, XX. New York: Charles Scribner's Sons.

—— (1908b) "A Text-Critical Apparatus to the Book of Esther," in R. F. Harper, F. Brown, and G. F. Moore (eds) *Old Testament and Semitic Studies in Memory of William Rainey Harper, II*, Chicago: University of Chicago Press.

Peristiany, J. G. and Julian Pitt-Rivers (eds) (1992) *Honour and Grace in Anthropology*, Cambridge: Cambridge University Press.

Pitt-Rivers, Julian (ed.) (1977) *The Fate of Shechem or The Politics of Sex: Essays in the Anthropology of the Mediterranean*, Cambridge: Cambridge University Press.

Radday, Yehuda T. (1990) "Esther with Humour," in Yehuda T. Radday and Athalya Brenner (eds) *On Humour and the Comic in the Hebrew Bible*, Sheffield: Almond Press.

Rashkow, Ilona N. (1990) *Upon the Dark Places: Anti-Semitism and Sexism in English Renaissance Biblical Translation*, Sheffield: Almond Press.

Register, Cheri (1975) "American Feminist Literary Criticism: A Bibliographical Introduction," in J. Donovan (ed.) *Feminist Literary Criticism*, Lexington: University Press of Kentucky.

Ringgren, Helmer (1956) "Esther and Purim," *Svensk Exegetisk Årsbok* 20: 5–24.

—— (1958) "Das Buch Esther," in *Das Hohe Lied, Klaglieder, Das Buch Esther* (with Artur Weiser), Göttingen: Vandenhoeck & Ruprecht.

Roustang, François (1990) *The Lacanian Delusion*, Oxford: Oxford University Press.

Sasson, Jack M. (1987) "Esther," in R. Alter and F. Kermode (eds) *The Literary Guide to the Bible*, Cambridge, MA: Harvard University Press.

Schneider, Jane (1971) "Of Vigilance and Virgins," *Ethnology* 9: 1–24.

Schwartz, Avraham and Yisroel Schwartz (1983) *The Megilloth and Rashi's Commentary with Linear Translation: Esther, Song of Songs, Ruth*, Jerusalem: Feldheim.

Sedgwick, Eve Kosofsky (1985) *Between Men: English Literature and Male Homosocial Desire*, New York: Columbia University Press.

—— (1990) *Epistemology of the Closet*, Berkeley: University of California Press.

Silverman, Kaja (1983) *The Subject of Semiotics*, Oxford: Oxford University Press.

Stanton, Elizabeth Cady *et al.* (1895) *The Woman's Bible, Part I*, New York: European Publishing Company.

—— (1898) *The Woman's Bible, Part II*, New York: European Publishing Company.

Streidl, Hans (1937) "Untersuchung zur Syntax und Stilistik des hebräischen Buches Esther," *Zeitschrift für die alttestamentliche Wissenschaft* 55: 73–108.

Suleiman, Susan Rubin (1991) "Writing Past the Wall or the Passion According to H. C.," in Hélène Cixous (Deborah Jenson, ed.), *"Coming to Writing" and Other Essays*, Cambridge, MA: Harvard University Press.

Talmon, Shemaryahu (1963) "'Wisdom' in the Book of Esther," *Vetus Testamentum* 13: 419–55.

Taylor, Mark C. (1994) "Denegating God," *Critical Inquiry* 20: 592–610.

Todd, Janet (1988) *Feminist Literary History*, London and New York: Routledge.

Torrey, Charles C. (1944) "The Older Book of Esther," *Harvard Theological Review* 37: 1–40.

Vattimo, Gianni (1992) *The Transparent Society*, trans. D. Webb, Parallax. Baltimore: Johns Hopkins University Press.

Walfish, Barry (1993) *Esther in Medieval Garb: Jewish Interpretation of the Book of Esther in the Middle Ages*, Albany: SUNY Press.

White, Sidnie Ann (1989) "Esther: A Feminine Model for Jewish Diaspora," in P. L. Day (ed.) *Gender and Difference in Ancient Israel*, Minneapolis: Fortress Press.

—— (1992) "Esther," in Carol A. Newsom and Sharon H. Ringe (eds) *The Women's Bible Commentary*, Louisville: Westminster/John Knox.

Wiesel, Elie (1979) *The Trial of God*, trans. Marion Wiesel, New York: Schocken.

Yamauchi, E. M. (1980) "Was Nehemiah the Cupbearer a Eunuch?" *Zeitschrift für die alttestamentliche Wissenschaft* 92: 132–42.

INDEX